Copyright, 1961, by Public Affairs Press
419 New Jersey Avenue, S.E., Washington 3, D. C.

Printed in the United States of America
Library of Congress Catalog Card No. 61-15691

INTRODUCTION

In this study Dr. William Manger writes with the authority of one who has devoted most of his life to the service of the oldest international organization of our times. There is probably no one in the hemisphere who has such a thorough knowledge of the political institution created by the nations in this part of the world to provide the machinery for conducting their relations in close collective cooperation. He entered the Pan American Union as a very young man, and through study, ability, and an intelligent utilization of his experience, he steadily rose until he achieved the high office of Assistant Secretary General of the Organization of American States.

I have known few instances of such complete dedication to furthering the aims and purposes of an international organization as that of Dr. Manger. As an aide to Dr. L. S. Rowe, who for so many years held the post of Director General of the Pan American Union, and later as Assistant Secretary General of the OAS, Dr. Manger attended almost all the important inter-American conferences from 1923 on. It is safe to say that there is no basic document in the history of the modern inter-American system in whose formulation Dr. Manger has not participated. In his capacity as Secretary of the Council of the OAS he witnessed, and on not a few occasions took part in the most complicated discussions on the application of the juridical standards laid down by the inter-American conferences. No one was better qualified than he to interpret a text on the basis of its background, its origin, its motivation, its intent. Dr. Manger's understanding of the history of inter-American relations of the last forty years is not only intellectual, but something also sensitive and human. Such is his consecrated devotion to the inter-American organization that his biography is almost inseparable from episodes in the history of relations between the countries of the Hemisphere.

It is with such authority that Dr. Manger has written this book, which is part history, part criticism, and a wholly acute and extremely clear political analysis of the positions of the different governments—particularly that of his own country, the United States—in the long period that has elapsed between the Congress of Panama of 1826 and President Kennedy's statements at the beginning of 1961. The conciseness and the soundness of Dr. Manger's observations are the natural result of the long and deep thought that he has given to the subject, of having foreseen numerous dangers, of having sought to prevent the commission of not a few errors, and of possessing a wealth of information on all the currents of opinion in every country in the hemisphere. And these are qualities natural to one whose only other activity outside the OAS has been his association with Georgetown University in this same field of inter-American relations.

Although this book is the product of a specialist and is designed mainly for those with some knowledge of the complexities of the inter-American system, it will be invaluable for any one who wishes to familiarize himself with the historical background and the present status of the regional organization that seeks to cover the whole field of international relations of the twenty-one countries of the Hemisphere.

At times Dr. Manger's impatience at the inefficiency or the impotence of the system is only too evident, his impatience at the slowness of its procedures, at the indifference of governments and their representatives to avail themselves of the instrument that could render more significant services if it were utilized more fully and to greater purpose. It is evident, too, that he is concerned over the very serious disease that afflicts international organizations: bureaucratization. When he was an official of the Organization, Dr. Manger constantly resisted the inroads of this plague, a plague that grows and is nourished both by the delegations of the several governments through a reluctance to impose restraints on an organization on which the governments are constantly making increasing demands; and by the organization itself with an international staff that, because it has as many chiefs as there are associated governments, does not have adequate responsibility and accountability and which, therefore, in the face of the indecision of the States, becomes an organ that produces innocuous papers, unnecessary documents, recommendations to which no one pays attention, all this with no sense of mission, no sense of the urgency of the task, and no sense of common purpose.

But notwithstanding these weaknesses of the institution, this study of Dr. Manger's makes it clear that, even with its debilitating slowness of development, the international organization of the Americas has a progressive history of surprising efficacy. Any one who examines for the first time what manner of thing the OAS is, can not fail to reach the conclusion that while the American nations have devoted more than a century to perfecting a working instrument with limitless possibilities to govern their relations within an order of law, they still do not make sufficient use of it. This is at once heedless and dangerous, for if the Organization should fail, there is no other system of inter-American relations that could replace it. The American States have vested a great deal of what is called their "sovereignty" in this Organization because they do not have any other machinery through which to handle their political relations, as might occur among the states of Europe. The crisis that Dr. Manger examines in his book cannot, therefore, be resolved except by new and great decisions and by positive action.

ALBERTO LLERAS CAMARGO

Bogota, Colombia

FOREWORD

"Pan America in Crisis," by its very title, reflects the current state of inter-American relations and of the inter-American regional organization. Pan America today is at the crossroads, and the direction it may take must be a matter of concern to every American Government and to every student of international relations. On the decisions that may be taken in the months and years immediately ahead may well depend the future of our Hemispheric system.

Events that are taking place today are not the consequence of what occurred only yesterday. They are the product of a long, evolutionary process that began a century and a half ago. Proposals advanced today by one government and the reaction of others to those proposals may be influenced by incidents that occurred a quarter, a half or even a century ago. And yet, although the problems may be different, the fundamental issue continues to be the same; namely, the formulation of policies and the implementation of programs that will promote the political, economic social and cultural development of the American Republics, and thus achieve the unity and solidarity of the Continent.

To appreciate the present, therefore, one must understand the past. The foundations of our Hemispheric system were laid by the great American Liberator, Simón Bolívar, when he convoked the Congress of Panama of 1826. Pan Americanism as it is understood today, embracing all the Republics of the Western Hemisphere, has been developing over a period of more than seventy years, since the First International Conference of American States met in Washington in 1889-90. The fortunes of the inter-American regional organization inevitably have fluctuated as the relations among the component states have changed and varied during this period.

The author of this incisive and penetrating study is well qualified to discuss the inter-American regional organization, its origin, development and present status. When my good friend, Dr. William Manger decided in 1958 to give up his certain re-election as Assistant Secretary General of the Organization of American States and to terminate his work at the Pan American Union, I felt sure that his interest in our regional system would not diminish. The publication of "Pan America in Crisis" confirms this assumption.

For forty-three years Dr. Manger was associated with the Pan American Union and the Organization of American States, as Assistant to the Director General and Counselor of the Pan American Union, and for the last twelve years of his career as Assistant Secretary General of the OAS. During this period of nearly half a century he also attended every important inter-American conference, and had an exceptional opportunity to know the organization, its possibilities and its limitations. It is understandable that among the Latin American representatives on the Council of the Organization he should have been known as "Mister Pan American Union."

Not everyone will agree with all his conclusions, and to some he may appear to be unduly criticial. But no one can question the sincerity of his views or the conviction on which they are based. This study appears at an opportune time and the views expressed therein may well be taken into consideration in the critical period that lies ahead.

HECTOR DAVID CASTRO

Washington, D. C.

CONTENTS

Chapter I

THE CURRENT CRISIS

"To our sister republics of the south, we have pledged a new alliance for progress—*alianza para progreso*. Our goal is a free and prosperous Latin America, realizing for all its states and all its citizens a degree of economic and social progress that matches their historic contributions of culture, intellect and liberty." This pledge of President Kennedy in his first State of the Union message is one of the few encouraging developments in the history of inter-American relations of the past decade. On its effective implementation will depend the future of the inter-American regional organization.

The words of the President are encouraging if for no other reason than that they reveal an awareness that all is not as it should be in our relations with Latin America. And the recognition of a situation is the first step in the adoption of remedial measures.

At the same time the pledge must be accepted for what it is—the first step in what of necessity must be a long, sustained undertaking. Remedial measures cannot be expected overnight. As the President observed in his Inaugural Address, speaking in another context, they will not be finished in the first one hundred days, nor in the first one thousand days, nor perhaps in the life of the administration that began in January of 1961. But if a start be made, the objectives will in time be reached.

The attainment of these objectives will require the combined efforts of all Western Hemisphere governments, as well as of the international institutions they have set up. In the fulfillment of the pledge, inter-American relations must be approached in their broadest aspect. The measures adopted must encompass not only our relations with the individual countries of Latin America, but our collective relations with all of them as represented by the Organization of American States.

It is to this last mentioned feature of inter-American relations that the present study is directed. It seeks to assess the role of the Organization of American States in the development of hemisphere relations; the rise and decline of the inter-American regional organization; and the extent to which the OAS may be capable of contributing

1

to the realization of the objectives envisioned in the new "alliance for progress."

The 1960's will be years of decision in the formulation of policies and the initiation of programs that will govern our relations with the twenty republics lying to the south of us; policies and programs that will either mark the end of a system of international relations that has developed through a long, slow and laborious process or, by reversing the downward trend of recent years, will restore inter-American relations to the high level they once occupied and that will re-establish the unity and solidarity of the community of American States.

International relations in the Western Hemisphere have been in process of development for a hundred and fifty years. In that span of a century and a half, dating from 1810 when the movement for independence began in Spanish America, there have been periods of friendship and understanding, of unity and solidarity; there have been others marked by misunderstanding and friction, of strife and conflict.

In recent years inter-American relations have deteriorated to one of the lowest levels in history. To find a comparable period when these relations were similarly strained and when the seeds of total disintegration were equally close to bearing fruit, it is necessary to go back nearly half a century.

Today, few of the elements that traditionally have served as the source of strength in the international relations of the nations of the Western Hemisphere are functioning as they should. The sense of political solidarity so laboriously built up in the years from 1930 to 1950 has gradually but steadily evaporated. The spirit of cooperation has deteriorated to such an extent that little or no progress has been made in solving the all-important contemporary problems of economic development and social improvement. The unity and solidarity of the American republics has been seriously undermined and the community of American States is rapidly becoming a fiction.

Among the nations of the Western Hemisphere international relations have long been conducted on several levels: one, the traditional bilateral, country-by-country approach; the other, the multilateral or the collective approach, represented at present by the Organization of American States.

The two methods are not exclusive, one of the other. Neither are they synonymous. There is an interrelationship between the two and each reacts upon and influences the other. And yet, the two are sufficiently dissimilar to permit the study of the one without a too detailed analysis of the other.

As an aspiration, an ideal, the inter-American regional system emerged in 1826; but its realization in the form of a system representing all the republics of the Hemisphere began only in 1890 when the First International Conference of American States met in Washington. The latest stage of its development dates from 1948, when the Charter of the Organization of American States was signed at Bogotá.

Is this latest stage the final one for the OAS? In the light of the existing situation and the course of events of the last few years, this question might well be asked, for as the OAS enters its eighth decade it is confronted by challenges greater than any it has heretofore faced. They go to the very heart of its existence as an effective international institution. On the organization's ability to meet these challenges will depend the justification for its future existence.

The OAS is faced by the challenge of mounting political tensions; tensions that began to manifest themselves in the Caribbean a decade ago and that recently have been building up at an accelerated tempo. As an institution that pretends to deal with international issues affecting the peace and security of the member states, the OAS has prided itself on its accomplishments during the past ten years. Its achievements in this area have been not without significance, especially in finding solutions to a series of minor incidents in the Caribbean area. But the tensions have tended to grow rather than to subside; their repercussions are now being felt throughout the Continent. It is not sufficient that the OAS should have been able to demonstrate a capacity to contend with the rivalries of opposing political leaders or to find temporary solutions to minor frontier incidents. Will it also be able to deal with the larger issues of peace and security that possess continental as well as intercontinental significance and are looming larger and larger on the international political horizon?

The OAS is faced by the challenge of economic development of twenty of its twenty-one members. The political issues that today confront the American States are largely an outgrowth of economic factors. Revolution, dictatorship, communism, democracy may make the headlines, but these are not the matters of continental import one might be led to believe from reading the daily press. The problem that is continental in scope and fundamental in nature is economic. Revolution and the threat of communism more often than not are the result of economic and social imbalances that exist in nearly every country.

The decline of markets and prices of basic commodities, the need for economic development, the effect of import quotas and controls on international trade—these are matters that confront all governments and touch all peoples.

It is the failure to find solutions to these problems that explains the present-day political stresses and strains that confront the nations of Latin America.

Coupled with the desire for economic development is the demand for social betterment. Throughout the Continent the spirit of reform is in the air. There is an irresistible determination to solve the long-standing social problems, to raise the standard of living, to narrow the gap that has traditionally separated the privileged few at the top and the underprivileged masses at the bottom. The attainment of this objective demands a strengthening of the economies of the several countries, a greater degree of stability in the markets and prices of basic commodities, and a program to diversify and broaden the bases of economic life.

In no land is this problem more clearly exemplified than in those of the Caribbean. Events in this area that are attracting so much national and international attention merely point up the nature and extent of the problem.

The Caribbean situation is not an isolated phenomenon. Neither is it a new one. What is occurring there today is a process that has been going on for the past ten years. It is a reflection and an intensification of a basic problem that presents itself throughout the southern part of the hemisphere, the urge for economic progress and social reform and the determination to achieve them.

For the United States, the Caribbean has added significance because the events are taking place in an area of our special interest and in such close proximity to our national territory. There, also, the problem is aggravated by the deep-seated antagonisms between the so-called champions of democracy on the one hand and the forces of dictatorship on the other. Equally significant, events in the Caribbean have revealed how quickly ideologies alien to the American concept of life are prepared to take advantage of every opportunity to create even greater difficulties, and how they threaten the very foundation of the hemisphere system.

What is happening in one country today happened yesterday in another. Tomorrow the urge for progress and reform may provoke an outburst in still another land. It is then, not a problem of Cuba,

Venezuela, the Dominion Republic or Chile.   It is a hemisphere problem, a matter of hemisphere concern.

If the Organization of American States is to justify its continued existence, it must demonstrate the ability to play its role and to make its contribution to the solution of these basic problems.   The annals of the Organization are filled with the debates and recommendations of conferences, councils and commissions, all largely unfulfilled.   The one constructive achievement in the economic area is the agreement establishing the Inter-American Development Bank.

The failure to find solutions to Western Hemisphere problems explains the decline and deterioration that has taken place in inter-American relations and in the prestige of the OAS during the past decade.   How long can the OAS afford not to produce a constructive and effective program of economic and social action?

Above all else, the OAS is confronted by the challenge to restore the unity and solidarity of the community of American States.   The greatest element of strength of the inter-American regional system is the ability of its members to work together in the solution of common problems and to act collectively on issues that may arise with nations in other parts of the world.   "America," it has been remarked, "is the Continent of peace, but it is also the Continent of solidarity."   Only to the extent that the member states can collaborate in solving the problems of each can they hope to achieve the solidarity to meet the collective problems of all.   The community of American States has been strongest when it has been able to count on the unity of all its member states; it has been weakest when its cohesion was dissipated.

During 1960 the defection of Cuba and the virtual ouster of the Dominican Republic reflect the loosening of the traditional bonds of continental unity and constitute a grave threat to the future of the inter-American regional system.   If such developments are permitted to continue, their corroding effects will serve further to undermine and weaken the structure of the Organization.   The re-establishment of continental unity and solidarity poses one of the greatest challenges to the Organization of American States.

The challenge to the OAS is at the same time a challenge to the member governments; a test of their sincerity and determination to make of the Hemispheric organization a viable institution.   The Organization is only what the governments are prepared to make it. The ability of the Organization to meet its challenges will depend in large measure on the policies and practices of the member governments, and on the capacity and statesmanship of the delegates they may appoint to implement these programs in the several representative organs of the organization. It is likewise a test of the ability, devotion, and dedication to service of the technical and administrative personnel who comprise the secretariats and agencies through which the Organization functions.

The challenge to the OAS and its member governments is, above all, a challenge to the United States. The future of the OAS—if it has a future—depends upon basic policies and decisions that this Government may make and the programs of action that it may adopt to govern its relations with the other nations to the south.

Do we want an OAS? Do we need an OAS? The immediate reaction is to answer this question in the affirmative. But a mere affirmation is not enough. An effective answer requires a complete change in our attitude of the past ten years, not only toward the Organization of American States, but to inter-American relations and to Latin America generally.

Economic development and social improvement are the focus upon which attention is now directed. But no less important than measures of a material nature is the need to recapture the spiritual values that are an essential ingredient of a strong and effective system of continental relations. In the period of greatest strength in Pan American relations the United States was able to present a program that captured the imagination of the masses of the Latin American people, that stirred their emotions, that convinced them of our sincerity of purpose and of our devotion and dedication to the basic principles that should govern the national and international life of people everywhere.

And thus it is that one of the great tragedies of the current era is that our ideological opponents should have been permitted to replace us in the imagination of so many of the Latin American people; to have created the impression in their minds that it is they, not we, who are the advocates of peace, the champions of democracy, the defenders of individual rights, and the friend of the oppressed and the downtrodden.

As Woodrow Wilson proclaimed a half century ago, and as Franklin D. Roosevelt so largely succeeded in doing several decades later, we must let it be known not only by words but also by deeds, that "we are the champions of democracy"; that we stand today as we have always stood for those basic principles of respect for human rights and human dignity on which our own country has become great, and that we are prepared to act and to collaborate with them in order that these principles may prevail throughout the American community.

CHAPTER II

ORIGIN AND BASES OF WESTERN
HEMISPHERE REGIONALISM

The inter-American regional system today functions principally through the Organization of American States, the Charter of which was signed at Bogotá, Colombia, in 1948, at the Ninth International Conference of American States. But that was merely the latest step in a long historical process.

To understand regionalism in the Western Hemisphere, the reason for its existence, the manner in which it has evolved, its present trend and future prospects, one must look far into the past. Regionalism has existed among the nations of the Western Hemisphere throughout their history, even before their emergence as independent states. It has found expression in every geographic area of the Continent: In Spanish America, in Portuguese America, in Anglo America and finally in the Continent as a whole.

Regionalism has manifested itself in several forms. It has existed as a centripetal force that brings together separate and distinct elements and finds expression in a spirit of cooperation, unity and solidarity. This is the sense in which the term is traditionally used in the discussion of international organization and relations.

But in the Western Hemisphere regionalism has also operated as a centrifugal force, a force that breaks up that which is joined together. In this sense regionalism expresses itself in a strong spirit of localism, a spirit that encourages every region, every community to be a power unto itself, unwilling to recognize or subordinate itself to any central authority or to any other region or community. It is a product of that intense individualism so predominant in the Spanish character, and the source of the strong feeling of nationalism that historically has dominated, and today is such an important factor in, the national and international life of most of the countries of Latin America.

In Spanish America both forms of regionalism were early and long in evidence. Among the Spanish colonies of the New World there was every reason why a sentiment of unity and solidarity should have existed. A common cultural heritage, three centuries of rule under the same form of government, similarity of language and religion, all

were conducive to giving to the colonists, widely scattered though
they were over immense distances, a community of interest and
similarity of outlook in meeting the common problems that confronted
them.

It is understandable, therefore, that a spirit of cooperation, a willing-
ness to make common cause with one another should very early have
appeared among the Spanish American colonies even while they were
yet under the control of the mother country. It was in the Wars of
Independence that this feeling found its earliest and, in fact, its highest
and noblest expression, especially in South America, when the people
of Argentina and Chile made common cause with one another, as did
those in Venezuela, Colombia and Ecuador. After their immediate
objectives had been achieved, they joined forces with those of Peru
in the final struggle for freedom.

For these reasons, also, the earliest attempts at the formation of a
regional association of states was a Spanish American initiative.
Although these moves sometimes broadened to include non-Spanish
speaking areas, the first attempts at regional organization were
Spanish American in origin and objective.

Given the strength of the influences that tended to unite the Spanish
colonies of the New World and the effective manifestation of the
spirit of unity and solidarity shown in their very emergence as independent states, many questions inevitably arise: Why were not the
earlier attempts at regional groupings more succesful? Why did not
a closer political union result? Why did not the Spanish colonies
associate themselves politically as did the English colonies of the
north and why were they less successful than the Portuguese of
Brazil in preserving their political and territorial unity? In short, why,
instead of a single Spanish speaking state, or at the most five or six,
did eighteen countries eventually emerge from the Spanish colonies
in the Western Hemisphere?

The answer is to be found on the other side of the coin of regionalism,
the existence of that negative, divisive characteristic of localism.
Much stronger than the centripetal influence that might have brought
the different segments of the Spanish colonial empire together, this
centrifugal force tended to divide and to separate them. The result
was a process of political and territorial disintegration. In Central
America, the Captaincy General of Guatemala broke up into five
separate states, each small, weak and politically unstable. In the
southern part of the Continent, the Viceroyalty of La Plata dissolved
into four separate political units. Even Simón Bolívar, despite his

prestige and influence, was unable to realize his ambition of a political confederation of the areas that he had been instrumental in freeing, and his Republic of Great Colombia soon disintegrated into its three component states of Colombia, Ecuador and Venezuela.

Not only did this divisive tendency prevent political integration, it also nullified the early attempts at the formation of a regional grouping of states. Considering the tremendous distances that separated them, the inadequacy of means of communication, not to mention the internal and external problems that confronted the various subdivisions of the former Empire, it was almost inevitable that political unity should have been unattainable. That the first attempts at regional association should also have failed is an indication of the strength of the feeling of localism.

But as the ensuing century was to demonstrate, an inherent sense of unity and solidarity has always persisted in Spanish America. On more than one occasion during the nineteenth century attempts were made to give this latent feeling tangible and concrete expression, usually in the face of political dangers that threatened from abroad. This sentiment has persisted down to the present day, notwithstanding the subsequent development of a continental movement of regionalism. It is frequently voiced by advocates of Pan-Latin Americanism as opposed to Pan Americanism, and recently has begun to find more tangible expression in the proposal for the economic integration of Latin America through the creation of a common market. Perhaps what the political problems of the nineteenth century were unable to achieve, the economic problems of the twentieth century may accomplish.

In Portuguese America Brazil's colonial heritage was basically the same as that of the Spanish colonies. The background of three centuries of rule under the same form of government, the similarity of language and religion, were factors that should have contributed to a spirit of understanding and cooperation, of unity and solidarity. And yet, in Brazil as in Spanish America, regionalism reflecting strong local tendencies also existed and on more than one occasion threatened the disruption and the break-up of the Empire into a number of Portuguese speaking nations. Through a fortunate combination of circumstances, including timely concessions to provincialism and the demand for greater autonomy in local administration, plus the national unifying influence of the monarchy, Brazil was able to preserve its political and territorial unity and to emerge as one of the largest and, potentially as well as actually, strongest states of the

Western Hemisphere. Actually, the preservation of their political and territorial integrity by the Brazilians was the expression of the highest form of regionalism, a regionalism that tends to bring together and to unite, rather than to separate and divide.

Although Brazil throughout its history has always shown a strong international outlook, there was little or no interest in a regional association of American States, as proposed several times during the nineteenth century. The international problems and relations of Brazil were different from those of the Spanish American republics. For Brazil, this was to be a development of later years.

In the historical development of Brazil and the United States there are many interesting parallels. In this country, also, regionalism in the hemispheric sense was conspicuously absent from early political thinking of the country and this government repeatedly disclaimed any interest in an association of American nations. But among the thirteen original colonies a spirit of regionalism definitely prevailed. As in the case of the Spanish American colonies, it first appeared in the struggle for independence, and it continued to assert itself as a centripetal force, first in the adoption of the Articles of Confederation and then in the Federal Constitution of 1789.

The spirit expressed in the slogan, "we must all hang together, or assuredly we shall all hang separately," was that which animated the revolutionary leaders of Argentina and Chile, of Venezuela and Colombia. They also realized that their own freedom was dependent upon the freedom of all South America, and that none of the freed colonies could consider itself secure so long as a nucleus of Spanish power remained on the Continent.

The feeling of regionalism among the thirteen English colonies was a very positive force. But, as in Brazil, at the outset and throughout the greater part of the nineteenth century, it did not extend beyond the immediate area of the newly created state. The experience of the pre-independence period, the embroilment in the colonial wars of the European powers, encouraged the determination to remain aloof from all entangling alliances, and discouraged participation by this government in the earliest proposals for the formation of an American regional association. Again, as in the case of Brazil, a sentiment for inter-American regionalism was to emerge in the United States only toward the end of the century.

In one form or another, then, regionalism has always existed in every part of the American Continent, from which it may be concluded that there is a natural basis for the inter-American regional system; that what exists in each of its parts must necessarily exist in the whole.

And yet there are not a few who question the validity of this assumption; who, on the contrary, contend that there is no solid foundation on which to justify the existence of Pan Americanism or the inter-American regional movement on a continental basis, and that it is founded on considerations that are wholly artificial or at least superficial.

Which raises the question: What is regionalism? What is a regional organization? Neither in the Charter of the United Nations nor in the Charter of the Organization of American States is a definition of regionalism to be found. Both contain an enumeration of principles and a statement of the nature and purposes of the organizations. In drawing up the Charter of the United Nations several attempts at definition were made, but, as finally adopted, Article 52 merely states that nothing in the Charter precludes the existence of regional arrangements or agencies for dealing with such matters relating to the maintenance of peace and security as are appropriate for regional action, provided such arrangements or agencies are consistent with the purposes and principles of the United Nations.

Perhaps it was just as well that no definition of what constitutes a regional agency was included in the basic charter of either organization. Definitions that have been attempted or descriptions that have been made usually predicate such movements on the premise of geographical contiguity, historical antecedents, similarity of political, economic, social and cultural interests and problems. These are elements that should and frequently do contribute to an understanding and a close relationship among states, but not necessarily so. They were all present in the early Spanish American attempts at union, league and confederation, and yet the attempts failed. It is frequently argued that they are not present in the inter-American regional movemen, and yet the system has been functioning for more than seventy years.

Regionalism, then, is not a matter of the existence or non-existence of certain definite physical or material characteristics. If a definition must be made it is advisable that it be as broad as possible, and that it be defined simply as a movement among a group of states desirous of cooperating with one another for the attainment of common objectives.

As the history of the inter-American regional system has amply demonstrated, more important than geography, language, religion, political organization, or cultural heritage, is the spirit that animates the member states. An essential ingredient to the success of a regional system is the existence of a community spirit, an ability to approach problems from the collective standpoint of the community as a whole and to seek solutions having in mind the welfare of all rather than the sole interest of the individual state.

When this spirit exists there is a logical foundation for a regional or, for that matter, any other international association of states. When this spirit is strong, the movement or the association is strong; when it is less in evidence, the movement is correspondingly weak. As Franklin D. Roosevelt expressed it when he was in the midst of giving practical application to his Good Neighbor policy: "It is a policy which can never be unilateral . . . It is a bilateral, multilateral policy and . . . the fair dealing which it implies must be reciprocated."

The need of this community approach to hemispheric relations is even more necessary today than it was a quarter century ago. The existence of this spirit is an indispensable requisite if Pan American relations are to develop on strong and solid foundations.

The inter-American regional system is not an isolated phenomenon. It does not function in a vacuum. It is an integral part of that large and complex mechanism that determines the relations among states and peoples. As such, it is influenced by the national attitudes of the several member states, by relations between the individual members, as well as by their relations with states and organizations in other parts of the world.

The former Secretary General of the Organization of American States and present President of Colombia, Dr. Alberto Lleras Camargo, often remarked that the inter-American regional system is no better and no worse than what the member governments are prepared to make it. The national attitude of every individual member state has to a greater or lesser degree influenced the fortunes of the Organization and the role that each state has played is, in itself, an interesting subject of study. Rarely have these attitudes followed a consistent pattern. On the contrary, they have tended to fluctuate as the national interests and policies of the respective states have changed and shifted.

Perhaps the most consistent of the national attitudes has been that of Argentina. It is a consistency of a negative rather than a positive character. The passive and frequently negative attitude of that country toward regionalism, except that which from time to time it has sought to foster in its own immediate area, developed in the first decades of the nineteenth century. It has been expressed on more than one occasion by the responsible political leaders of the country, and has consistently influenced its participation in the Pan American movement.

Brazil, on the other hand, is an example of a country whose attitude, certainly since the inception of the modern Pan American movement in 1890, has been uniformly sympathetic, as it has been to international cooperation generally. That of Mexico has varied. Although Mexico has never been indifferent, its participation in the activities of the inter-American regional system has tended to fluctuate. At times it has assumed a position of leadership in championing reform, and at others its participation has been characterized by an attitude of complacency and conformity.

To a considerable degree Mexico's attitude toward the regional movement has reflected the fluctuations in its bilateral relations with the United States. This, of course, is merely an example of a general situation. The inter-American regional system has tended to revolve to a large extent around the national policies of the United States, the policies and practices of this country with respect to the system itself, to the individual countries of Latin America and to the reaction of those countries to their bilateral relations with the United States. Certainly this has been true since the Pan American movement assumed continental proportions with the convocation of the First International Conference of American States in 1889. Even in the earlier Spanish American attempts of the nineteenth century at the formation of political associations, the national policies of the stronger neighbor to the north were an important factor in influencing the course of events.

But if national attitudes determine the success or failure of international organization, the history of the inter-American regional system also reveals the extent to which international organization, properly exercised, can influence the national policies of individual governments. The classic example of this interplay of forces is that afforded by the drastic revision in the Latin American policy of the United States, both multilateral toward the Continent as a whole and bilateral with respect to individual countries, that occurred during and in the years immediately preceding the enunciation of the Good Neighbor policy. The abandonment of the unilateral policy of intervention as practiced under the Roosevelt corollary to the Monroe Doctrine, the modification of the Wilsonian policy of recognition based on constitutionalism, and the liberalization of treaty relationships with individual countries of Latin America, all were consequences of the mounting tide of criticism that began to build up at the Pan American Conference of 1923 and that reached a climax at the Havana Conference of 1928. The almost unanimous condemnation voiced at that time of prevailing United States policy, particularly the practice of intervention, revealed the need of a re-examination and a revision which began almost immediately upon the adjournment of the Conference.

During the past ten years the Latin American countries similarly have been using the inter-American organization as a sounding board to induce changes in the economic policies of this country, so far, however, with little success. Whether the coming decade will witness changes in the economic field comparable to those that were introduced into the political field three decades ago, may be a test of survival for the inter-American regional system.

It is not only the bilateral relations of the United States with individual countries that have had an influence on the inter-American regional organization. The history of Pan Americanism reveals many other instances of the influence of bilateral relations on the progress of the movement. For many years the Tacna-Arica dispute between Chile and Peru which grew out of the War of the Pacific of 1879-1883 and was not finally settled until 1929, hung like a cloud over the deliberations of Pan American conferences. In addition to disrupting the relations between the two countries immediately concerned and those of South America generally, it effectively prevented even the first steps in the development of a continental system for the pacific settlement of disputes.

The rivalry that for so many years characterized the relations of Argentina and Brazil undoubtedly contributed to and has been reflected in the attitude of both countries toward the inter-American regional organization, serving to explain at least in part the traditional support always shown by Brazil and the lukewarmness of Argentina toward the movement. The absence of diplomatic relations between Mexico and the United States in 1923 led to Mexico's abstention from the Fifth Pan American Conference of Santiago, and marked the beginning of a debate that in time produced far-reaching changes in the organization of the Pan American Union and in the composition and direction of its Governing Board. And who will want to estimate the effect on the Organization of American States of the differences that began to develop between the United States and Cuba in 1960?

In the same manner that the inter-American regional system reacts to a multiplicity of factors within the Western Hemisphere, so also is it influenced by the relations of its members with nations in other parts of the world and with other international organizations.

Not infrequently there has been a tendency to equate Western Hemisphere regionalism with isolationism, and to conclude that the existence of an inter-American regional organization is incompatible with an effective world organization. Actually, the Western Hemisphere idea as a movement to isolate America from Europe or any other part of the world never existed and was never intended to exist. Undoubtedly it was designed to prevent the unwanted and the unwarranted interference of non-American states in the affairs of the Western Hemisphere, and the nations of America, from the time of Bolívar down to the present, have repeatedly expressed their views on this point. But it was never the intent to build an iron, silk or any other kind of curtain around the Hemisphere to isolate it from all contact with the outside world or to exclude other parts of the world from all association with the American Continent.

Such a narrow interpretation of inter-American regionalism may occasionally have been espoused by extremists in the United States, and at times may have been reflected in official declarations, especially in years prior to the creation of the United Nations and at the time of our aloofness from the League of Nations. But it was never the view of any significant number of individuals or governments of the inter-American community as a whole. On the contrary, the sentiment of the great majority of the member states of the inter-American regional system has always been for the maintenance of close ties with Europe and other areas of the world.

The countries of Latin America, likewise, have never seen the slightest contradiction between their inter-American regional organization and their participation in the world organization. At one time or another they were all members of the League of Nations, at the same time maintaining their membership in the Pan American system. In the formative stages of the United Nations, when there was not a little sentiment in this country for sacrificing the regional Western Hemisphere system to the One World concept of international organization, the Latin American countries became the strong champions of regionalism. There is, of course, no contradiction between the two. Each is a form of international association. The justification for the existence of either or both is their ability to contribute to the purposes for which they were established.

The inter-American regional system is not the sum total of international relations in the Western Hemisphere. It is only a part and, in the final analysis, a relatively small part of the totality of such relations. It represents the multilateral side of hemisphere relations, features that can be dealt with on a collective basis because they reflect the interest and affect the welfare of the community of American States.

The history of the last few decades has clearly revealed that the most effective contribution that the inter-American regional organization can make is to help create an atmosphere that will permit progress to be made on all levels, the bilateral and the multilateral, and in all areas, the political, the economic, the social and the cultural.

No less important than to know what such an organization can do is to realize what it cannot do. To presume to be more than it is, to undertake more than it is capable of performing — whether this presumption stems from the organization itself or from its member governments — is to render a distinct disservice not only to the cause of international organization but to international relations in general.

CHAPTER III

FROM PANAMA TO WASHINGTON

In the chronology of inter-American regionalism three dates stand out in bold relief. The first is 1826, the date of the Panama Congress convoked by the Liberator, Simón Bolívar; the second is 1889-90 when the First International Conference of American States met in Washington on the initiative of the United States; and the third is 1948, the year in which the Charter of the Organization of American States was signed in Bogotá, Colombia.

It is regrettable that so little attention has been given to the 1826 Congress of Panama, especially by North American students and historians. By many authors it is completely ignored; others brush it off as a premature, fruitless and poorly conceived attempt at the attainment of an impossible objective. If for no other reason than its position in the perspective of history and the growing importance of international organization during the twentieth century, it is deserving of greater attention than it usually receives. A more careful analysis of the Congress and the diplomatic negotiations that preceded it, might well reveal that they were not without some influence on the political and military events of the time.

In any evaluation of the Panama Congress it is necessary to look beyond the meeting itself. The Congress was not an isolated phenomenon. It was the climax of a series of diplomatic negotiations that began in 1822 and that had a two-fold objective: one, to complete and consolidate the struggle for independence; the other, to lay the foundations of a permanent political association among the newly established states. Examined within the context of this larger framework, the Panama Congress, and the events that preceded it, may not have been the fiasco or the futile gesture so often ascribed to it. Certainly, it constituted a precedent that was to be invoked on more than one occasion in the ensuing years and that even today exerts an influence on the national and international thinking of many Latin Americanists.

The five years preceding the 1826 Congress were years of doubt and uncertainty for the Spanish colonies in America. By 1822 they appeared to be well on the way to the attainment of their objective of independence. Southern and northern South America had been liberated, and in Mexico and Central America national governments had been set up. But Spanish resistance had not been completely overcome, especially in Peru. Spain not only refused to recognize the independence of the newly created states, she resisted all suggestions of compromise and gave every indication that she would avail herself of any aid that might be forthcoming to reconquer her lost possessions. In 1822 the intervention of the Holy Alliance in Spain appeared to be a possible prelude to further aid to help Spain. The possibility, unfounded though it may have been in the light of subsequent revelations, caused no little concern in Spainish America, as it did in London and Washington.

In London, the British Foreign Secretary, George Canning, proposed to the United States a joint declaration in which the two countries would declare that recovery of the colonies by Spain was hopeless, that recognition was a matter of time and circumstance, that neither country aimed at the possession of any portion of the former colonies, and that they could not see any portion of them transferred to any other power with indifference. At the same time conversations carried on with the French Ambassador produced the Polignac Memorandum, in which England gave notice that she would recognize the Spanish American states if there were any interference by the Holy Alliance in the conflict between Spain and the colonies.

In the United States the British proposal gave rise to extensive consultations within the administration and with former Chiefs of State, eliciting from Thomas Jefferson the prophetic statement made in his response to the consultation of President Monroe: "The question presented by the letters you have sent me is the most momentous which has ever been offered to my contemplation since that of independence. That made us a nation, this sets our compass and points the course which we are to steer through the ocean of time opening on us."

The result of the consultations was not a joint declaration with England, but the Monroe Doctrine, a unilateral declaration in which the United States asserted that the American continents were henceforth not to be considered as subjects for future colonization by any European powers, and that any attempt on the part of the latter to extend their system to any portion of this hemisphere would be considered as dangerous to our peace and safety.

Spanish American preoccupation in 1822 had to do with the immediate objective of independence and the long range objective of

political association. It found expression in two treaties which Colombia, under the leadership of the Liberator, Simón Bolívar, began to
negotiate in 1822 with each of the other Spanish American states.
In the first treaty the parties entered into a military alliance whereby
they mutually agreed to take such measures as might be necessary to
sustain their independence of Spain and of every other foreign dominion. In a second treaty it was agreed that an inter-American congress
should be held in Panama, at which a multilateral agreement would be
drawn up embodying the principles of the bilateral treaties of alliance,
and at the same time there would be created a confederation establishing close political ties among the newly liberated states.

Which of these three initiatives was most effective in discouraging
intervention by the Holy Alliance and thus achieving the immediate
objective of assuring the independence of the Spanish American
states? On one occasion George Canning is reported to have remarked
that he had brought the New World into being in order to redress
the balance of the Old. In his instructions to the American delegates
to the Panama Congress of 1826 Secretary of State Henry Clay remarked that the proclamation of the Monroe Doctrine had served to
discourage any idea of interference by the Holy Alliance in the affairs
of the Spanish American states and had thus achieved the immediate
objective of the Congress.

But is it not possible that the diplomatic negotiations initiated by
Bolívar in 1822 and the resulting treaties of alliance may also have
had some effect on the existing political, diplomatic and military
situation? After all, the independence of the Spanish American states
was largely the product of their own efforts and the treaties of alliance
could well be interpreted as a reaffirmation of their determination not
to be deprived of the fruits of victory.

The Holy Alliance may never have been the real threat to the
Spanish American states that it at one time appeared to be, and to
meet that danger perhaps none of these initiatives was necessary. But
if Henry Clay could give himself a pat on the back, and if George Canning could boast that his intervention brought forth the New World,
perhaps at this late date a degree of credit might be given to Bolívar
and his bilateral treaties of alliance for discouraging any intention
that might have existed of European intervention in the final stages
of the Spanish American struggle for independence.

Whatever the reason, whether it was the Monroe Doctrine, the
Polignac Memorandum, or the measures taken by the Spanish Americans themselves, by the time the Panama Congress convened in 1826

the general international situation had changed considerably from what
it had been in 1822. The battle of Ayacucho had been fought and the
last Spanish forces had been compelled to surrender. The independence
of the Spanish American States had been recognized, not only by the
United States but also by Great Britain and other governments. The
danger from the Holy Alliance, if it ever existed, had definitely dis-
appeared. The immediate objective of the Panama Congress and the
negotiations leading up to it had been achieved.

It not infrequently happens in the life of nations as of individuals
that, as danger from without tends to recede, differences from within
tend to rise. By 1826 the need for military alliances, and even more
so for a political confederation, appeared far less necessary than in
1822. The spirit of military cooperation and political association was
replaced by that divisive tendency that even at this early date had
begun to find expression in Spanish America. Doubts and misgivings,
suspicions and jealousies, began to enter into the preparations for the
Congress and to influence participation in it. Was the real objective
of the Panama meeting, it was asked, to place Spanish America under
the hegemony of Colombia? In the expected campaign to liberate
Cuba, was the leadership to be assumed by Colombia or Mexico? Following the island's liberation, into which country was it to be incorporated? Would the decision to transfer the Congress to Tacubaya place
it too greatly under the influence of Mexico, and thereby lessen the
prestige of Colombia?

Inevitably, such sentiments, doubts and misgivings had their effect.
They explain partly the limited participation in the Congress, particularly the absence of Argentina and Chile. Only four countries were
represented, Central America, Colombia, Mexico and Peru, although
these represented ten of the present day Spanish American Republics.
Great Britain and the Netherlands had observers, and although the
United States had accepted the invitation, neither of its representatives
arrived at the Congress.

Under the best of circumstances, the long-range objective of Bolívar
of a closely knit political federation would have been foredoomed to
failure. It was too ambitious, too unrealistic and visionary for the
conditions then prevailing. The centrifugal forces of localism and
disintegration had already begun to operate, and even before the
Congress formally convened the sentiments of the delegates had
changed. The original idea of a federation with broad political authority delegated to a General Assembly had been rejected. The Treaty
of Union, League and Confederation that came out of the Panama

meeting was essentially a mutual assistance pact. But even this went farther than the member states were prepared to go, for Colombia was the only state to ratify. Panama was a century and a quarter ahead of the times.

Any sense of security that may have been engendered in the minds of the Spanish Americans by the final success of the Wars of Independence and the recession in the threat of the Holy Alliance, was soon dissipated. The new states soon found themselves confronted by other problems, internal and external. In the ensuing three decades the precedent of Panama was to be invoked on more than one occasion to seek collective action to deal with the dangers that threatened their peace, security and political independence.

As one reviews the history of Spanish America during the first half of the nineteenth and in fact well into the second half, one wonders how they were able to survive the numerous problems that confronted them. During this period most of the countries were merely drifting, without direction, aimlessly, like a disabled ship.

Internally, as Francisco García Calderón, the Peruvian historian, so vividly describes it in his study: *Latin America: Its Rise and Progress*: "The first period of independence is troublous, but full of color, energy and violence . . . South America is ruled by ignorant soldiers, the evolution of her republics must therefore be uncertain. There is no history properly so-called, for it has no continuity; there is a perpetual *ricorso* brought about by successive revolutions; the same men appear with the same promises and the same methods. The political comedy is repeated periodically: a revolution, a dictator, a program of national restoration. Anarchy and militarism are the universal form of political development."

Externally, the Spanish American republics during the first three or four decades of their national statehood, were confronted by dangers that not only threatened their peace and security but jeopardized their very existence as independent states. As J. Fred Rippy succinctly puts it in his history of Latin America: "War vessels of all the major powers moved menacingly along the coasts and often blockaded ports or bombarded coastal towns and cities." In not a few instances these activities went beyond mere threats and took the form of outright intervention and territorial acquistions.

The experience of the Spanish American republics in consolidating their independence in the nineteenth century affords an interesting comparative study with that of the new states of Africa entering the national arena in the twentieth century. Under the watchful eye of a sympathetic world opinion, with the support of the international organization, and with two great rival power blocs vieing with one another in the political and economic aid which they can render, the situation of the emerging states of Africa is in striking contrast to that of Spanish America a century ago, confronted as it was by continuous problems within and constant dangers from without.

For many years the attitude and the policy of Spain continued to pose a danger to the states that were her former colonies. She long remained unreconciled to their loss and refused to acknowledge their existence as independent states. The process of recognition was not begun until several decades after it had become an accomplished fact, and was not finally completed until well toward the end of the century. Coupled with the latent threat implicit in the unwillingness to grant recognition, were the positive steps taken by Spain on several occasions to reassert her claims to portions of her former Empire. In 1860 Santo Domingo was reincorporated as a part of Spain and remained so until 1865; in 1864 a Spanish naval force occupied the Chincha Islands off the coast of Peru and for a time posed a threat to the west coast countries of the Continent; in 1862 Spain participated with France and Great Britain in the intervention in Mexico; and earlier, in 1848, the Spaniards offered aid to the political exile Juan José Flores in return for his assistance in restoring Spanish authority in northwestern South America.

These first decades in the national life of the newly established states of Spanish America were also marked by the French and English blockades of the Rio de la Plata in the years from 1838 to 1850; by the British occupation of the Falkland Islands in 1830, the incorporation of Belize as a British Crown Colony and the extension of British influence along the Mosquito coast in Central America; the French bombardment and occupation of Veracruz in 1838, and the more serious threat arising from the French invasion of Mexico in 1862, preceded by the English, Spanish and French blockade of the Gulf ports of Mexico and followed by the establishment of the Maximilian Empire under French protection from 1863 to 1867.

Not only from Europe but also from their northern neighbor were the newly established Spanish American states confronted by threats and dangers. The early period of close and friendly relations had arisen from the sympathy and support extended by the United States to the Spanish American colonies in their struggle for independence, the circumstance that this country was the first to extend recognition to the independent governments, and the proclamation of the Monroe

Doctrine in 1823. Now this friendship was rudely shattered by the Mexican-American War of 1845-47 and the ensuing drive of the United States toward its "manifest destiny."

The effect of these developments on United States-Latin American relations are bluntly described by Jesús M. Yepes, Colombian student of inter-American relations, in the following words:

"The predatory expeditions of the filibusterer Walker against Nicaragua; the imperialist war of the United States against Mexico in 1847, under the guise of a questionable interpretation or defamation of the Monroe Doctrine which culminated in the dismemberment of the Aztecan republic and the loss of some of its most flourishing provinces; and the policy of 'manifest destiny' which then made its appearance in some influential spheres of North American public opinion, aroused a growing uneasiness in the Latin American peoples. Justly alarmed by the dangers to their security and territorial integrity which these phenomena of international policy implied, the Latin American republics again turned their thoughts to the warnings that Bolivar had given in the last years of his life when he exclaimed: 'Unite, America, for if you do not anarchy will devour you.' "

We are still living under the impact of this unfortunate period in our relations with Latin America. It is a heritage that we are not permitted to forget and which continually rises to plague us.

In this atmosphere of danger that appeared to be closing in from all directions and threatening their very existence, the Spanish American states, as Yepes observes, turned to the Bolivarian concept of collective action and invoked the precedent of Panama. On two occasions representatives of Spanish American states met in Lima, Peru, the first time from December, 1847 to March, 1848, and again from November, 1864 to March, 1865. The Treaty of Union and Confederation signed at the first meeting and that of Union and Defensive Alliance signed at the second were essentially political in character and emphasized the need of collective action for mutual defense. In between these congresses, in 1856, diplomatic representatives of Spanish American states, meeting in Santiago and in Washington, signed treaties of alliance and confederation aimed at the same objective.

Like those of Panama of 1826, none of the treaties was productive of practical results, for they were not ratified and never became effective. But again, as in the case of Panama, the question arises: Were these treaties wholly without value? Is it not possible that the sentiment of unity and solidarity that they reflected might have had some effect on the events out of which they arose, and the dangers at which they were directed?

The brusque dismissal of these early political conferences as complete failures may be too harsh, too unfair an estimate. Basic conditions had not changed between 1826 and the dates of these later meetings and any hope that they might produce a close political association continued to be wholly visionary and unrealistic. Inevitably the treaties failed of ratification. But perhaps the Congresses, by the mere fact that they were held, did serve a purpose and by the example that they gave of unity and solidarity did help to preserve the political independence and territorial integrity of the participating states.

The decade from 1860 to 1870 was a period of crisis for the Western Hemisphere. The European interventions in Santo Domingo, in Mexico, and along the west coast of South America constituted a danger unequaled since that posed by the Holy Alliance in 1822. Actually, it was greater, for it was real and positive whereas that of the Holy Alliance was only potential. In the United States, the intersectional strife that threatened to rend the nation, made it impossible for this government at the outset to do more than register diplomatic protests at the repeated violations of the Monroe Doctrine.

Consequences of this period might well have been disastrous, but as not infrequently happens the long-range effects were beneficial. As history was to reveal, this decade of crisis marked the end of one and the beginning of another period in inter-American relations.

On the one hand the 1860s were destined to be the high water mark in European interventions and attempts at reconquest. These were not yet a thing of the past, as witness the Venezuelan incidents of 1895 and 1902. But they were never again to assume the ominous proportions of this earlier period.

In the United States, the Civil War preserved the Union. It also changed national attitudes. With the abolition of slavery the spirit of manifest destiny so strongly in evidence in the two decades preceding the Civil War and that aroused such grave misgivings throughout Latin America, tended to lose its appeal. As Samuel Flagg Bemis expresses it in his admirable work *The Latin American Policy of the United States*: "Following the Civil War there had come a sag of indifference, nay even positive reaction, to expansion in any direction, whether advocated by President Johnson and Secretary Seward, or by President Grant and Secretary Fish, whether in Canada or Cuba or the Virgin slands. The purchase of Alaska — a one-man job for

which Seward was almost solely responsible — and the occupation
of the Midway Islands in the Pacific Ocean were all that the people
of the United States would then tolerate of these ambitious plans of
the new Republican apostles of Manifest Destiny."

At the end of the century it is true there was a final burst of
territorial expansion as a result of the Spanish American War and the
acquisition of the Panama Canal Zone, but these acquisitions were a
consequence of a new form of manifest destiny and not inspired by
a mere desire to acquire territory.

In the United States also, the European interventions in the Western
Hemisphere at a time when we were involved in our own Civil War
served to give renewed emphasis to the Monroe Doctrine and to
make it the cardinal principle of American foreign policy. Again to
quote Bemis: "At first the words of Monroe had been no more than
a paper no-trespassing sign to Europe: hands off the New World!"
After the Civil War, in the words of Dexter Perkins, the Monroe Doctrine became "a true national dogma, endorsed by all parties, awaken-
ing an instantaneous response in the breasts of patriotic Americans."

In Latin America, the unpleasant experiences of so many of the
republics with European powers during the years when we were unable to do more than give lip service to the principles of the Monroe
Doctrine, also induced a revision of attitude toward the United States.
Despite the doubts and misgivings engendered by the territorial
expansion of the United States following the Mexican War, not a few
Latin Americans now began to realize that Europe constituted for
them a more serious danger, and that perhaps the United States might
be a source of support and protection for them.

These events, in the words of Francisco Cuevas Cancino, Mexican
author of a study on the history of the inter-American regional
movement, caused the Latin Americans to open their eyes. "In their
attitude toward the United States and Europe," he goes on to say,
"the Spanish Americans began to reveal a greater sense of understanding . . . There is no longer the panic fear of the 40s, but a more exact
appreciation of their historic significance, and if they continued to look
with a wary eye on the colossus of the north, they were not unmindful
of the benefits they had derived from its power. It had become clear
that Europe had lost the power to impose its will on the New World.
The determination of the people to preserve their freedom had been
clearly established in Mexico as well as in Santo Domingo. Independence was an established fact, and the Spanish Americans were
convinced that Europe knew it."

The events of this significant decade were destined to have far-reaching effects on the inter-American regional movement as well. Not only did they affect the relations of the Latin American countries with Europe and induce them to modify their attitude toward the United States; they also influenced the relations among the Spanish American states themselves. The recession in the threat of European intervention and reconquest gave to the Latin American countries a feeling of security greater than they had possessed at any time since the Wars of Independence. At the same time it took away the one influence that heretofore had been the motivating force behind the movement of regionalism. Fear — of reconquest and of intervention, of foreign attempts against their independence, security and territorial integrity — had been the basis of the Panama meeting of 1826, of the two Lima Congresses of 1848 and 1864, as well as of the Santiago and Washington treaties of 1856. With the greater security they began to feel in the second half of the nineteenth century, regionalism as it had previously found expression, lost its motivating force. No further meetings inspired by these considerations were destined to be held, for there was no need for them. For all practical purposes, regionalism as heretofore practiced had come to an end.

The resulting vacuum was partially filled by two juridical congresses held in 1878 and 1888 to codify principles of law, but if regionalism was to become a significant factor in the international life of the Western Hemisphere new forces and new elements had to be found. This void was filled when, on invitation of the Government of the United States, representatives of eighteen nations of the American Continent met in Washington on October 2, 1889, in the First International Conference of American States. Regionalism in the Western Hemisphere had assumed continental proportions.

Chapter IV

FROM WASHINGTON TO BOGOTA

The International Conference of American States that met in Washington from October 2, 1889 to April 19, 1890, opened a new chapter in Western Hemisphere regionalism. It likewise marked the beginning of a new concept in international organization.

The 1889 conference had been preceded by an earlier attempt to hold such a meeting. In November of 1881 Secretary of State James G. Blaine extended invitations to the governments of the independent states of America to meet in Washington one year later "for the purpose of considering and discussing the methods of preventing war between the nations of America." This invitation was subsequently withdrawn, due to changes in the administration of the government in Washington following the death of President Garfield and the unfavorable political situation in Latin America.

It is readily understandable that literature in English on the Pan American movement since 1890 is more extensive than on the earlier or historical period. For Pan Ameircanism as it has developed during the past seventy years originated on the initiative of the United States, and its fortunes have largely revolved around the policies, and at times the lack of policy, of this Government.

Despite the relative wealth of material, however, the inter-American regional system lends itself to more detailed analysis than it has thus far received. It offers a rich field of study and investigation: from the standpoint of its physical growth and development; the juridical changes and the process of internationalization through which it has passed; and, of course, the results that have marked its activities in the various areas to which it has directed its attention. A chronological study of the successive conferences that have marked the history of the movement may appear to be a monotonous repetition of discussions and decisions on the same subjects, but an analysis would reveal the areas in which inter-American relations have advanced, stood still or, in some instances, retrogressed.

Furthermore, as previously observed, regionalism in the Western Hemisphere does not operate in a vacuum; it is influenced by the multiplicity of factors — national, bilateral and multilateral — that determine the attitude and affect the relations of governments and peoples. It lends itself, therefore, to studies on the role of individual governments in the affairs of the organization and, conversely, the extent to which the organization has at times influenced the policies and practices of individual governments. Nor should there be overlooked the relationship of the inter-American regional system and its member states to other international organizations and to states in other parts of the world.

Physical Growth

The circumstance that the nations of the Western Hemisphere should have met in conference in 1889 was not in itself unique. Conferences had been held previously, among the American States as well as in other parts of the world.

Neither was there anything unusual in the creation by the Conference of an International Union of American Republics or in the establishment in Washington of a Commercial Bureau through which that Union was to function. Other international institutions had been set up at other conferences, such as the Universal Postal Union and the International Telegraph Union.

What was unique was the continuity that resulted from this initial meeting; something had been started that, although unknown at the time, was destined to carry on. No less unique was the new concept that gradually evolved with respect to the manner in which an international institution should be organized and administered. This evolutionary process can best be observed by following its application to the Commercial Bureau, forerunner of the present day Pan American Union, and to what is today the Council of the Organization of American States. Today, these two agencies are the hub around which the inter-American system in large measure revolves.

The Conference of 1889-1890 and the Commercial Bureau of the American Republics were obvious experiments. No one knew whether a second conference would ever be held. The Commercial Bureau had been set up for ten years and before this period had expired more than one government had expressed an intention to withdraw.

The cynical might contend that the creation of the Bureau was the first attempt in the Western Hemisphere at bureaucracy on an international level and that, the seed having sprouted, it would never be uprooted but inevitably would continue to grow and grow. On the other hand, the international minded can derive no little satisfaction from the statement found in the 1895 Annual Report of the Director of the Commercial Bureau that "the officials of the International Union have accepted responsibility beyond that of citizens and officials of a single republic. They are representatives of a political entity unique in its nature and based upon the highest ideals — that of extending friendly relations between peoples animated by a common desire for the development of the principles of self-government and of individual liberty on this Continent." If not the first, this certainly was one of the earliest references to the spirit that should animate the personnel of an international organization, the spirit of the international civil servant. It is worthy of the most advanced concept of international organization even today. Inspired by such a sentiment an international institution can be really effective; without it, it becomes merely a bureaucracy.

In its physical characteristics, the agencies and instrumentalities through which it functions, the inter-American system, like Topsy, just "growed." Unlike international organization on the world level — the League and the United Nations — which were the product of carefully worked out, pre-arranged blueprints, what is today the Organization of American States during the first half century of its existence developed on the basis of improvisation.

From the First International Conference of 1889-90 and the Commercial Bureau of the American Republics, new institutions were established from time to time and additional functions entrusted to those institutions already existing.

In 1902 the Pan American Sanitary Bureau was established as a result of a decision taken at the Second International Conference in Mexico, thereby becoming the first of the technical or so-called specialized organizations in the inter-American regional system. Subsequently, other technical agencies were created to function in other areas of activity on a permanent, continuing basis, including the Pan American Child Institute at Montevideo in 1927; the Inter-American Commission of Women with its seat at Washington in 1928; the Pan American Institute of Geography and History at Mexico in 1929; the Inter-American Indian Institute at Mexico in 1940; and the Inter-American Institute of Agricultural Sciences at Turrialba, Costa Rica, in 1944. These today comprise the six specialized organizations that function within the framework of the Charter of the Organization of American States.

The question will doubtless arise in many minds as to why the specialized agencies under the Charter of the Organization of American

States should be made up of such a diverse and heterogeneous conglomeration of institutions. An agency to function in the field of
public health is understandable, as likewise in agriculture. But why,
the question might be asked, should there be a specialized organization
for child welfare, women, geography and history, or, for that matter,
Indians, despite the considerable aboriginal population to be found
in many parts of the Continent. The answer is to be found in the
circumstances and the conditions under which they were created.
Some were established in response to special interests or pressures;
others to meet immediate problems of the moment. Once established,
they tended to perpetuate themselves and, being able to satisfy the
conditions laid down in the Charter for classification as specialized
organizations, they have been blanketed into the inter-American regional system.

Not all of these agencies, of course, are of equal importance. Some
are relatively small and play a correspondingly minor role, not only
in the over-all work of the inter-American regional system but in their
ability to contribute to the immediate problems for which they were
set up. A few are international more in name than in substance.
Organizationally, the permanent offices of several of these so-called
international institutions partake more of the nature of national de-
pendencies, with a personnel made up almost entirely of nationals of
the countries in which they have their seats. Their only international
feature is that they derive financial support from several countries and
that, periodically, they sponsor conferences or meetings at which
delegates from Pan American countries are in attendance.

The Commercial Bureau of the American Republics, as its name
implies, was originally set up in 1890 to compile trade statistics and
to disseminate information on consular regulations and customs procedures. Gradually it was entrusted with additional functions.

By the Mexico City conference of 1902 it was authorized to publish
pamphlets, maps, topographical and geographical charts and other
documents. In 1906, at the Third Conference of Rio de Janeíro, the
dissemination of information on educational matters was included in
its list of purposes. More significant in influencing its growth was the
practice that developed as early as 1902 of entrusting it with the
implementation of conference resolutions or, as the resolution of the
Buenos Aires Conference of 1910 expressed it, "to carry into effect all
resolutions, the execution of which may have been assigned or may
hereafter be assigned to it by the International American Conference."
As the agendas of the conferences gradually broadened, there was

virtually no subject, political or social, that in time did not come within the Bureau's sphere of interest. Coupled with the responsibility of preparing documentation for the International Conferences and serving as the custodian of their archives, it became in a very real sense the central and permanent organ and the general secretariat of the organization.

In order that its title might more accurately correspond to its functions, the name was changed in 1902 from Commercial Bureau to that of International Bureau of the American Republics, and in 1910 to that of the Pan American Union.

As the area of inter-American activity broadened the practice soon developed of convening specialized conferences to deal with problems of a specific and usually a technical character. The Pan American Sanitary Conference that met in 1902 and created the Pan American Sanitary Bureau was the first of what in time became a list of several hundred specialized conferences dealing with every conceivable type of problem, political, economic, social and cultural.

To supplement the activities of the permanent agencies, numerous *ad hoc* councils, commissions and committees were set up. As early as 1906 at the Third Conference of Rio de Janeiro, steps were taken toward the formation of an International Law Commission, forerunner of the present day Inter-American Council of Jurists and the Inter-American Juridical Committee, to undertake the codification of international law. The Inter-American Economic and Social Council, today, with the Council of Jurists and the Cultural Council, one of the three technical organs of the Council of the Organization of American States, had its origin in 1939 in a resolution adopted at the First Meeting of Consultation of American Foreign Ministers to deal with the economic and social problems arising out of World War II. An earlier counterpart of this agency was the Inter-American High Commission, set up in 1915 to study the economic problems resulting from World War I.

Likewise a product of the second World War is the Inter-American Defense Board, established pursuant to a resolution adopted at the Third Meeting of Consultation at Rio de Janeiro in 1942. The draft Charter of the Organization of American States contemplated an Inter-American Defense Council as a fourth technical organ of the Council of the Organization, but opposition from several delegations at the Bogotá Conference limited action on this proposal to the creation of an Advisory Defense Committee to meet with the Organ of Consultation when circumstances warrant. So far the Committee has never been convoked, although the Inter-American Defense Board continues as the Secretariat of the Committee and as the organ of preparation for collective self-defense.

One of the anomalies of international organization in the Western Hemisphere was that for more than half a century this conglomeration of conferences, councils, commissions, and institutions existed without a collective name and with no clearly defined interrelationship or interdependence. The resolution of the 1890 Conference formed what it presumed to call an International Union of American Republics and subsequent resolutions on the Pan American Union spoke of a Union of American Republics. But this was never construed as a name applicable to the system as a whole, and even less was it interpreted as implying an association or union in the political sense of the term.

Despite inconveniences, the looseness and informality that characterized this earlier form of organization had some advantages. For one thing it was an organization based largely on resolution, and the resolution of one conference could be modified by a resolution of a succeeding conference. There existed, therefore, a degree of flexibility in meeting new situations that does not exist in a treaty form of organization. But it had the distinct disadvantage of being dispersed over a large number of separate instruments, with no clear indication of the relationship among its several parts.

To remedy this defect the preparation of an organic charter was undertaken to incorporate in a single document the norms and principles that govern the inter-American regional system and the instrumentalities through which it functions. The Charter of the Organization of American States was signed at Bogotá, Colombia in 1948 at the Ninth International Conference of American States. The Charter contains little that is new; it is essentially a work of codification. Its principal advantage is that, with this one document and cross-reference to one or two others, it is possible to determine with reasonable accuracy what the inter-American regional system is.

The Process of Internationalization

Not the least interesting feature of the Pan American movement since its establishment on a continental basis in 1890 is the process of internationalization through which it has passed, reflected particularly in the successive steps that have been taken in the organization and direction of what is today the Pan American Union and the Council of the Organization of American States. These steps, that in time transformed both agencies into international institutions in the true sense of the word, afford an interesting study in international organization.

As originally conceived, perhaps reflecting the limited experience of the time, the Commercial Bureau of the American Republics when it was set up in 1890 was placed wholly under the supervision of the Secretary of State of the United States. It was he who organized the Bureau, and it was he who appointed the Director and the personnel. Initially, also, the Annual Reports of the Director of the Bureau were submitted to the Congress of the United States. The Bureau had more of the characteristics of an agency of the United States Government than of an international institution.

But the process of internationalization was not long in starting. Responding to the pressure of some of the other member countries and, probably, to the views reflected in the Director's 1895 Annual Report, a meeting in 1896 of the Secretary of State and the diplomatic representatives in Washington of the Latin American countries resulted in the appointment of a permanent executive committee of five countries with the Secretary of State as Chairman *ex officio,* to act as a board of supervision and administration of the Bureau, including the selection and appointment of the personnel.

This was the first step in the internationalization process. In 1902 the responsibility of organization and administration devolved upon all the member governments with the creation of the Governing Board of the International Bureau of the American Republics, predecessor of the present Council of the Organization of American States. As the resolution of the Mexico City Conference expressed it, this Board "shall consist of the Secretary of State of the United States, who shall be its Chairman, and the diplomatic representatives of all the Governments represented in the Bureau and accredited to the United States of America." Although constituting a definite step forward in the process of internationalization, the resolution of 1902 was construed, and increasingly so with the passage of time, as possessing two inequalities: the first, with respect to the composition of the Board, limiting the freedom of action of the member states in appointing their representatives and making representation contingent upon diplomatic relations with Washington; and the second, by permanently entrusting the chairmanship to a single country. Nevertheless, this set-up continued for two decades.

It not infrequently happens that it is not the realities of a situation

that count, but the interpretations that can be drawn from surface ap-
pearances.   The circumstance that the Secretary of State of the
United States was the permanent chairman of the Board in all
probability had no other significance than a courtesy to the Foreign
Minister of the country in which the Board had its seat. Today,
Pan American conferences invariably are presided over by the Foreign
Ministers of the countries in which they are held. But the mere fact
that this was written into the basic statute of the Governing Board
created an appearance of inequality that in time reflected unfavorably
on the institution as well as on the United States.

In 1923 Mexico did not have diplomatic relations with the United
States and consequently had no representative on the Governing Board
of the Pan American Union. One of the functions of the Board, then
as now, was the preparation of the programs of the International Conferences of American States, and as Mexico had taken no part in the
formulation of the program of the Fifth Pan American Conference
she took the position that she could not participate in the conference
that met in Santiago, Chile, in that year.

Although no Mexican representative was present, the issue raised
by the absence of Mexico was very much in the minds of the delegates
at the conference. At Santiago, three decisions were taken which
definitely liberalized and broadened the international character of
the organization. The first was to the effect that the governments of
the American Republics enjoy, *as of right,* representation at the International Conferences of American States and in the Pan American
Union. This principle was later incorporated in the Charter of the
Organization of American States and assures to every member state
the right to participate in the activities of the organization without
regard to the state of its diplomatic relations with other members.

The Conference also agreed that in the future the Governing Board
should elect its Chairman and Vice Chairman. As events were to
prove, this was merely a gesture, for the Secretary of State continued
to serve as Chairman of the Board. For twenty years the Board
went through the formality each year of electing the Secretary of
State as Chairman, rotating, however, the post of Vice Chairman. In
the opinion of many this practice lent credence to the frequently
voiced impression that in a Board made up of diplomatic representatives and the Secretary of State, the former would give priority to
their diplomatic responsibilities before the government to which they
are accredited and, as a matter of courtesy and of good politics, choose
the Secretary of State to preside.

As early as this 1923 Conference a proposal was made to vest the government of the Pan American Union in a Board composed of representatives "accredited to the Pan American Union," rather than the host country. This, however, was twenty years ahead of the times. Due principally to the opposition of the United States, the farthest the Conference was able to go was a decision permitting a government to appoint a special representative on the Board in the absence of a diplomatic representative in Washington. The United States objection to specially accredited representatives was based on the belief that it would be "unwise and impracticable to set up in Washington a separate political body to deal with Pan American affairs and to which diplomatic agents might be accredited." Reflecting the vagaries of national and international politics, this same argument was advanced in 1948 by some Latin American delegations against granting political powers to a Council with its seat in Washington.

What had been proposed at Santiago in 1923 became a reality in 1945 when, at the Inter-American Conference on Problems of War and Peace, held at Chapultepec, in Mexico, it was agreed that the Governing Board of the Pan American Union should be composed of *ad hoc* delegates, who "shall not be a part of the diplomatic mission accredited to the government of the country in which the Pan American Union has its seat." But this requirement was too extreme for some governments, which objected to the maintenance of two missions in Washington. Although the decision had been reached at an important diplomatic conference, consultations conducted subsequently among the governments resulted in a modification making it optional for them to appoint either special ambassadors or their Washington accredited diplomatic representatives to serve on the Board.

At Chapultepec it was further agreed that the Chairman of the Governing Board should be elected annually and that he should not be eligible for re-election for the immediately succeeding period.

Related to the foregoing decision on the composition and direction of the Governing Board was another having to do with the administrative officers, the Director General and the Assistant Director, of the Pan American Union. Although not specifically set forth in the resolution on the organization of the Union, custom had always decreed that the Director General should be a North American and the Assistant Director a Latin American, and that both could serve indefinitely. At Chapultepec it was decided that both officers should be chosen for ten-year terms, that they should be ineligible for re-election, and that they should not be succeeded by persons of the same nationality.

In 1948 these principles were substantially embodied in the Charter of the Organization of American States. The one change that was introduced permitted an incumbent Assistant Secretary General to be re-elected. The process of internationalization had come a long way since the bases of organization laid down at the first Conference of 1890.

Powers and Functions

No less interesting than the composition of the Council, in tracing the historical development of the inter-American regional system, is the question of the powers and duties that should be entrusted to it. To an even greater extent it reflects the attitude of the member governments toward international organization, and particularly the extent of the authority they are prepared to delegate to such an agency, especially one with its seat in Washington.

As originally set up at the Mexico City Conference of 1902 the duties of the then Governing Board were wholly administrative. These are functions that it continues to perform today as the Council of the Organization of American States in fulfillment of Article 51 of the Charter making the Council responsible for the proper discharge by the Pan American Union of duties assigned to it. Interestingly enough, its powers in this regard were originally much broader than they are today, for by the terms of the 1902 resolution it not only supervised, it actually administered; the appointments to all positions were made by the Board and signed by the Chairman.

The practice of the International Conferences of entrusting to the Governing Board the implementation of resolutions and recommendations, inevitably led to a broadening of the Board's authority. It gradually undertook to deal with matters that extended far beyond the administration of the Pan American Union. Eventually the question arose as to how far this authority should go, and specifically whether it should encompass the exercise of political powers.

The term itself—"functions of a political character"—is vague and indefinite. It has never been precisely defined and doubtless means different things to different people. Composed as it is of representatives appointed by governments, every action of the Council has political overtones and in a sense implies the exercise of political powers. What is apparently meant is the intrusion of the Council in

questions that may present themselves between two or more governments, issues that relate to the political conduct of states in their
relations with other states.

The issue first arose in 1928 at the Sixth International Conference
at Havana. Reflecting the sentiment that then prevailed, the American Republics there agreed that neither the Governing Board nor
the Pan American Union should exercise functions of a political character. But in the ensuing years the atmosphere and the attitude under-
went a gradual change. Partly by force of circumstances and partly by
a growing feeling of confidence, the Board began to play a larger
role in the political affairs of the Continent.

On the one hand, in the development of the inter-American system
of collective security that slowly and laboriously was being constructed
during the decade of the thirties, the Governing Board almost imper-
ceptibly was required to intervene in order to make the machinery of
consultation function; there was no other instrumentality that could
do so. The Board thus became associated with the procedure of
consultation almost from the very outset and in spite of the prohibition
against the exercise of political functions.

In addition, the spirit of continental unity and solidarity that had
been engendered in the period immediately preceding and during
World War II had carried enthusiasm for the regional system, particularly in Latin America, to its greatest heights. At a time when in the
United States attention was directed to the formation of the United
Nations and when the One World idea was so strongly fixed in the
minds of policy makers in this country, there was an equally strong
sentiment for the regional organization among the other member
states.

As a result, when the Chapultepec Conference of 1945 was held,
the Governing Board of the Pan American Union was given authority
greater than it had ever before possessed. In the resolution on the
reorganization, strengthening and consolidation of the inter-American
system, the Board was empowered to take action "on every matter
that affects the effective functioning of the inter-American system
and the solidarity and general welfare of the American Republics."

Vague as the terminology may sound, this was an authority of far-
reaching significance. The right to act in matters affecting "the solidarity and general welfare" was designed to give to the Governing
Board broad political powers, in contrast to the purely administrative
functions previously assigned to it. As the Director General of the
Pan American Union observed in his report on the Conference: "At

Mexico City the Pan American Union was transformed by the adoption of rules making it the central agency of the system, with full power to undertake the most difficult tasks and with absolute freedom to carry them out properly."

The spirit of Chapultepec of 1945 that prompted this broad delegation of authority carried over to the Inter-American Conference for the Maintenance of Continental Peace and Security held at Rio de Janeiro in 1947 and found expression in the Inter-American Treaty of Reciprocal Assistance.

By the terms of this treaty, today one of the pillars of the inter-American regional system, the Governing Board of the Pan American Union was given a key role in the Western Hemisphere collective security system. It was made the provisional organ of consultation, empowered to act until the Ministers of Foreign Affairs of the American Republics could assemble as the principal organ of consultation; it was named the agency that receives and passes upon requests for the convocation of the Organ of Consultation whenever the peace and security of the Continent are threatened; and it was also recognized as the liaison agency between the inter-American system and the world organization in matters of peace and security.

Without doubt the Rio Treaty and the Chapultepec Conference represent the high water mark in the historical development of the inter-American regional system. By the time the Ninth International Conference of American States met at Bogotá in 1948, at which the Charter of the Organizatin was drafted, a recession in the high tide of Pan American unity and solidarity had set in. It is interesting to speculate on what the effect might have been on the far-reaching powers given to the Governing Board if the Rio Treaty had been negotiated the year after instead of the year before the Bogotá Conference of 1948.

Two moves were made at Bogotá to undo what had been done at Chapultepec and at Rio, and to take away from the Council the broad political powers entrusted to it. With respect to the Rio Treaty proposals were made and actively supported for the creation of a new organ of consultation, one that would have its headquarters in one of the other American Republics or that would rotate from capital to capital every five years as designated by each Inter-American Conference. When it was realized that such a modification would involve a revision of the Rio Treaty and a repetition of the laborious process of ratification, that suggestion, although supported by a number of influential delegations, did not prosper. The Rio Treaty was permitted to stand as originally drafted and the Council of the Organization was permitted to exercise the powers entrusted to it by the treaty. As the subsequent applications of the Rio Treaty were to show, these were broad powers indeed, and the one function that may be said to have justified the existence of the Council.

But the Bogotá Conference was determined that no additional political authority should be delegated to the Council of the Organization. As the Minister of Foreign Affairs of Mexico expressed it, he was not disposed to turn the clock backward, but neither was he prepared to push it forward. In reality, however, the Conference did take a backward step. The broad delegation of authority given to the Council in the Chapulepec resolution of 1945, to take action on every matter that might affect the solidarity and general welfare of the American Republics, was rescinded. Instead, by the terms of Article 50 of the Charter as it came out of the Conference, the Council was authorized to take cognizance only of those matters referred to it by the Inter-American Conference or the Meeting of Consultation. It is a distinction between a general and a specific grant of powers; instead of an authority to act when it considers it necessary, the Council now acts only when specifically authorized to do so.

The question inevitably arises as to the reason for this abrupt and emphatic change of sentiment. Perhaps it was due to the resurgence of the spirit of nationalism, a factor that has manifested itself throughout the history of the Pan American movement. Perhaps it was revealed, with a frankness rarely witnessed in Pan American discussions, in the remark of a Chilean delegate when he said that "it is not appropriate that all American activities have their seat in Washington."

There is a lesson to be learned from these incidents of history. The question might well be asked whether that lesson has yet been fully learned. It is a lesson that should be kept constantly in mind in the further process of the organization, direction and administration of the inter-American regional system.

Substantive Activities: Peace and Security

In its seventy year history the inter-American regional organization has dealt with a great variety of subjects in every field of activity— political, economic, social and cultural. With some it has had greater success than with others. On many of these subjects there is sufficient material so that a separate thesis could be written. Peace and security may be cited to illustrate the manner in which the regional system has dealt with two of the basic problems that have come before it: peace, originally the sole objective in initiating the modern Pan American movement, when Secretary of State Blaine in 1881 invited the American States to meet in Washington to discuss methods of preventing war between the nations of America; security, because it is the primary objective of the national and international policy of every country and an indispensable requisite for any system of international organization.

The acceptance of the principle of continental responsibility for continental security is the major accomplishment of the inter-American regional organization up to the present time. Curiously enough, it is the one subject that had the greatest difficulty in getting off the ground, so to speak; but one which, once the initial step had been taken, quickly accelerated to extraordinary heights. It marked the realization in the second quarter of the twentieth century of the hopes and aspirations that prompted Bolivar to convoke the Congress of Panama a century and a quarter earlier.

The succesive steps in the development of the collective security system emphasize the evolutionary character of the inter-American regional movement; the patience, persistence and perseverance that are required in reconciling divergent points of view and the national interests of twenty-one different states. It likewise reflects the strong interplay of forces that influence relations among the member states of the inter-American community; the manner in which the collective view of the community can frequently influence the policies and practices of individual governments, and the extent to which collective action must frequently be modified to satisfy individual points of view.

The inter-American collective security system is the direct outgrowth of the acceptance of the principle of non-intervention. The 1928 Sixth Pan American Conference of Havana, while not the most important in the long series of inter-American conferences, was not without significance. The immediate results were essentially negative, but it definitely marked the close of one chapter in the history of Pan American relations and, by that very fact, compelled the opening of another if the movement was to continue.

The great controversial issue before the Havana Conference was the practice of unilateral intervention as exercised by the United States since 1903 under the Roosevelt corollary to the Monroe Doctrine. Responding to the almost unanimous sentiment of opposition voiced at the Conference, this practice was abandoned, and in 1933 and again in 1936 the American Republics signed agreements embodying

the principle that no state has the right to intervene in the internal
or external affairs of another. Obviously, an alternative procedure
had to be developed, a substitute had to be found for the practice that
had heretofore prevailed.

The first step in the development of a multilateral collective security
system was taken in 1936 at the same conference in which the un-
conditional protocol of non-intervention was signed. At the Inter-
American Conference for the Maintenance of Peace, held in Buenos
Aires, the American Republics declared that "every act susceptible
of disturbing the peace of America affects each and every one of them,
and justifies the initiation of the procedure of consultation." In the
Convention for the Maintenance, Preservation and Re-establishment
of Peace, it was also agreed that "in the event of war or a virtual state
of war between American States, the Governments of the American Republics . . . shall undertake without delay the necesary mutual consultations, in order to exchange views and to seek . . . a method of peaceful collaboration; and, in the event of an international war outside
America which might menace the peace of the American Republics,
such consultation shall also take place to determine the proper time
and manner in which the signatory states . . . may . . . cooperate to
preserve the peace of the American Continent."

By these agreements the principle of consultation, the procedural
basis of collective action whenever the peace and security of the Continent are threatened, had been accepted. But the mechanism through
which the consultations should be conducted had yet to be devised.
This step was taken in 1938 when, at the Eighth International Conference of American States held in Lima, Peru, it was agreed that
the consultations should be carried on by the Ministers of Foreign
Affairs of the American Republics meeting in their several capitals by
rotation and without protocolary character.

The substantive parts of this agreement are worth quoting. In the
Declaration of Lima the American Republics announced that "in
case the peace, security or territorial integrity of any American Republic is theatened by acts of any nature that may impair them, they
proclaim their common concern and their determination to make effective their solidarity, coordinating their respective sovereign wills by
means of the procedure of consultation . . . using the measures which in
each case the circumstances may make advisable. It is understood
that the Governments of the American Republics will act independently in their individual capacity, recognizing fully their juridical
equality as sovereign states."

Words more vague, obscure and ambiguous, expressed with greater circumlocution could hardly have been devised. They reflect the importance of the subject under consideration and the difficulty of reconciling conflicting national points of view. Specifically, the imprecise terminology of the Declaration of Lima was a concession to the traditional Argentine attitude toward regional commitments. As the Argentine Foreign Minister who headed his delegation at the Conference expressed it, "we do not require special pacts." And he added: "American solidarity is a fact that no one does or can question. Each and everyone of us is ready to sustain and support that solidarity against any danger that from whatever source may threaten the independence or the sovereignty of any State in this part of the world." Undoubtedly he had a point. If that spirit exists it is stronger than any formal agreements. But the Foreign Minister in resisting acceptance of a formal commitment of collective action for mutual assistance was merely expressing the historical Argentine attitude toward inter-American pacts of this nature. Such sentiments had been voiced by Mariano Moreno as far back as 1810; by Rufino de Elizalde, Foreign Minister at the time of the preparations for the Second Lima Congress of 1864; by Roque Saenz Peña, who headed the Argentine delegation to the First International Conference of American States of 1889-90 and later became President of the Republic; and by Argentine delegates to Pan American conferences of a more recent era. In other words, the negotiation of inter-American agreements on fundamental isues is a long, slow and laborious process. It is not something that can be accomplished overnight.

The wisdom and the foresight of the authors of this new force in inter-American relations was revealed sooner perhaps than the architects themselves anticipated. Within less than a year after the Lima Conference, following the outbreak of war in Europe, the first Meeting of Consultation of American Foreign Ministers was held in Panama in August, 1939. At that time emphasis was on neutrality, on keeping belligerent activities away from American shores, by the delineation of a zone around the Western Hemisphere to be kept free from the commission of hostile acts by the belligerent nations.

As the war's course changed so did the inter-American attitude toward the conflict. In July, 1940, shortly after the downfall of France and the conquest of the Netherlands, the American Republics met in a Second Meeting of Consultation in Havana. There they proclaimed their opposition to the transfer of existing European possessions in the New World from one non-American sovereignty to another and their determination to assume jurisdiction over these areas themselves should such a move be made. This was the application on a continental scale of the no-transfer principle first laid down by the United States as far back as 1811.

At this same meeting there also appeared the first specific mention of the principle of reciprocal assistance in the event of aggression. In a resolution that attracted little attention at the time, the Foreign Ministers declared that "any attempt on the part of a non-American state against the integrity or inviolability of the territory, the sovereignty or the political independence of an American State shall be considered as an act of aggression against the States which sign this declaration."

There is nothing in the record to indicate that the signers of the declaration themselves were aware of its far-reaching implications. The proposal was introduced by the Foreign Minister of Venezuela and only the representatives of Colombia and Chile formally recorded that the assumption of obligations and responsibilities such as those implied in this resolution were contingent upon approval by the appropriate national organs in accordance with established constitutional norms.

Following the attack on Pearl Harbor in December, 1941, the Havana resolution became the basis of collective action by the American Republics in World War II. Interestingly enough, it was the Foreign Minister of Chile who invoked the resolution and proposed that a Third Meeting of Consultation be held to consider the measures that should be taken in the light of the aggression on the United States. The Meeting of Consultation that met in Rio de Janeiro in January, 1942, not only reaffirmed the principle of reciprocal assistance, but also proposed that all the American Republics give it practical application by breaking diplomatic relations with Japan, Germany, and Italy.

Here again the inter-American regional organization was faced with the problem of reconciling collective community action with individual national attitudes. The resolution adopted at Rio de Janeiro suffered from the same vagueness and ambiguity that marked the Lima Declaration of 1938. As originally presented by Colombia, Mexico, and Venezuela the draft resolution recommended in categorical terms the severance of diplomatic relations with the aggressor states, but in the interest of finding a formula acceptable to all delegations the language was modified to read that such action shall be taken by each Republic "in accordance with the procedures established by their own laws and in conformity with the position and circumstances obtainable in each country in the existing continental conflict." Such language can mean all things to all people and to the Argentine government, and to a lesser extent Chile, justified the delaying tactics that characterized their compliance with the recommendation. Given the situation that existed in Argentina at the time, fulfillment of the terms of the Rio resolution, no matter how emphatically expressed, would have been difficult to obtain. Unfortunately, also, the attention that was later focussed on Argentina's war attitude served to overshadow the extraordinary example of continental unity and solidarity that marked the conduct of all the other states of the inter-American regional system toward the war effort.

As World War II drew to a close the principle of collective security and reciprocal assistance was not only reaffirmed by the American Republics but was given broader scope at the Inter-American Conference on Problems of War and Peace that met at Chapultepec, in Mexico, in February, 1945. Previous instruments had been directed solely against the danger of aggression from non-continental sources, but the Act of Chapultepec was made to apply to aggressor states within the Continent, as well as to states or groups of states outside the Hemisphere. For the first time, furthermore, specific provision was made for the application of sanctions, and the Act enumerated the measures that might be taken against an aggressor.

The Act of Chapultepec was a war measure, and its far-reaching provisions embodied in a simple resolution were made possible by the authority that had been vested in the several governments for the purpose of the war effort. In order that the principles and procedures of the Act might be made a permanent part of the international law of the Continent, it was agreed that they should be embodied in a treaty which the American Republics would ratify in accordance with their established constitutional procedures.

The result was the Inter-American Treaty of Reciprocal Assistance, signed at Rio de Janeiro in September, 1947, at the Inter-American Conference for the Maintenance of Continental Peace and Security. Like the Charter of the Organization of American States, the Rio Treaty also is essentially a work of codification. It reproduces, in permanent treaty form, the basic principles and procedures enumerated for the first time in the Havana resolution of 1940, reiterated in the Rio resolution of 1942, and expressed in greater detail in the Act of Chapultepec of 1945.

As its name implies, the Rio de Janerio Treaty of 1947 is primarily an instrument of collective security and reciprocal assistance. In the

development of the structure of the inter-American regional system it
was contemplated that the Rio Treaty should be supplemented by a
continental treaty on pacific settlement, an agreement that would
afford an ample mechanism to the American Republics to settle by
peaceful means any controversy that might arise among them. But the
negotiation and the general acceptance by all the American Republics
of a continental treaty on the peaceful solution of controversies has
been even a slower process than that of collective security. In fact,
it is an objective that has not yet been attained.

In this area it is possible again to observe the extent to which
national attitudes can influence and retard the attainment of continental objectives. Of all the subjects that have appeared on the
agendas of Pan American conferences none has been considered more
often or discussed more exhaustively than that of pacific settlement.
As already observed, it was the basis of Secretary Blaine's original
invitation in 1881 and it has appeared on the programs of most Pan
American conferences held since then.

Early failure in this field was due to the clash of national interests
between Chile on the one hand and Peru and Bolivia on the other.
The War of the Pacific, which was still in progress between these three
countries in 1881, was one of the reasons for the postponement of the
first Washington Conference. Thereafter, the long unsettled Tacna-
Arica dispute between Chile and Peru hung like a cloud over inter-
American relations for the first four decades of the modern Pan American movement. For a time it encouraged a "balance-of-power" trend
in South America, and it effectively nullified every attempt at early
inter-American conferences to deal with the subject of arbitration and
conciliation.

Pacific settlement was on the agenda of the 1889 Washington Conference, not, however, with the thought that the conference would sign
a definitive treaty, but merely that it would discuss and "recommend
for action" a plan of arbitration. The draft treaty that was drawn up
was not signed within the conference, but by eleven delegations meeting
on the outside.

So strong was the national attitude of Chile against the consideration
of any plan that might even remotely be construed as requiring
the submission to arbitration of the issue pending with Peru that, at
Mexico City in 1902, the Chilean delegation threatened to withdraw
from the conference if such a treaty were submitted for signature.
As a result, the treaty that was drawn up was signed by nine delegations outside the Conference. It is not surprising that instruments

drafted in such an atmosphere and signed under such circumstances should have been ratified by only a small number of states and never became significant factors in the international relations of the American Republics.

These incidents reflect the manner and extent to which continental agreements and progress on a continental scale are subject to the specific situations of individual countries. It has been well observed that the international movement cannot proceed faster than the member governments are prepared to go. This view was well expressed by the great Brazilian diplomat and statesman Joaquim Nabuco, when he presided over the Third Pan American Conference at Rio de Janeiro in 1906: "... the great object of these conferences should be to express collectively what is already understood to be unanimous, to unite, in the interval between one and another what may have already completely ripened in the opinion of the Continent, and to impart to it the power resulting from an accord among all American nations. This method may appear slow, but I believe it to be the only efficacious one, the only way of not killing at its inception an institution which is worthy of enduring throughout the centuries."

No real progress in the development of a continental peace system could be made until the Tacna-Arica dispute was solved. It was not finally settled until 1929, but in 1923 it appeared to be well on the road to solution when the procedural aspect of the problem was submitted to the arbitration of the President of the United States. Although this attempt proved abortive, it did make possible the signing in 1923 at the Fifth International Conference of American States in Santiago of the Inter-American Treaty to Avoid or Prevent Conflicts, the first general treaty of pacific settlement to come out of a Pan American conference. The high sounding title of the treaty was out of proportion to its intrinsic worth, for it merely provided for committees of investigation to report on the facts of disputes, with no authority to propose or suggest solutions. But it did constitute a start, and after the definitive settlement of the Tacna-Arica issue in 1929, other agreements rapidly followed: The Conciliation Convention and the Arbitration Treaty of 1929; the Additional Protocol to the Conciliation Convention of 1933; and the Treaties on Good Offices and Mediation, on the Prevention of Controversies, and on the Maintenance, Preservation and Re-establishment of Peace, all signed in 1936 at the Buenos Aires Peace Conference.

Collectively, these agreements afforded every facility for the orderly settlement of differences. But because they were all separate instruments, some of which were ratified by some governments and not by others and none of them by all the twenty-one governments, their effectiveness was considerably curtailed. Coordination and consolidation thus became not only desirable but necessary if an effective continental peace system was to be achieved. Proposals to this effect were advanced as early as 1936 at Buenos Aires and again in 1938 at the Eighth Pan American Conference in Lima, and finally culminated in the American Treaty on Pacific Settlement signed at the Ninth International Conference of American States at Bogotá in 1948. This Treaty embodies in a single instrument all of the procedures scattered through the six or seven previously negotiated, including good offices and mediation, investigation and conciliation, judicial procedure and arbitration.

Curiously enough, the Inter-American Peace Committee is not mentioned in the Bogotá Pact, due to the fact that when this consolidated instrument was drawn up the resolution creating the Peace Committee had been forgotten. The Committee originated in a 1940 resolution of the Second Meeting of Foreign Ministers, which recommended the creation of a five-member committee charged with "the duty of keeping constant vigilance to insure that States between which any dispute exists or may arise . . . may solve it as quickly as possible, and of suggesting . . . the measures and steps which may be conductive to a settlement." It was not until the Bogotá Conference had adjourned that the 1940 resolution was resurrected and the Commitee constituted. The Committee was destined to play a more active role in inter-American relations than any of the procedures set forth in the formal continental treaty of pacific settlement.

The Inter-American Treaty on Pacific Settlement, the Charter of the Organization of American States, and the Inter-American Treaty of Reciprocal Assistance constitute the three pillars on which the modern structure of the inter-American regional system rests. They were expected to afford a complete mechanism for the effective functioning of the organization. How well they have served their purpose is to be determined from an examination of the manner in which the Organization of American States has functioned in the years since 1948.

CHAPTER V

THE OAS SINCE BOGOTA

Who would have predicted in 1948 that within the short span of twelve years political, economic and ideological differences would develop among American States to such an extent as to undermine the foundations and threaten the very existence of the inter-American regional organization?

Who would have believed that within that brief period inter-American relations would have deteriorated to a level where the chief of state of one nation would be accused of complicity in an attempted assassination of another, that an investigating committee of the Council of the Organization would find these charges sufficiently well grounded to justify a Meeting of Consultation, and that the American Foreign Ministers would unanimously recommend the breaking of diplomatic relations and the imposition of sanctions?

The Ninth International Conference of American States climaxed a series of meetings and a fifteen year period of cooperation that had placed inter-American relations at the highest level in history. The future of the inter-American regional system looked exceptionally bright. The Charter of the Organization, the Inter-American Treaty of Reciprocal Assistance and the American Treaty on Pacific Settlement, it was felt, afforded all the machinery required to deal with any problem that might arise. As far as could be foreseen, the twenty-one American republics had achieved a system of continental relations whereby, through the collective action of all, they were in a position to make positive contributions to the progress of each and to the welfare of the community of American States.

But this bright hope soon proved to be illusory. The measure of success of any international organization is the current state of relations of its members. Among the American Republics these in 1960 were low indeed. Nor was this a sudden and unforseen development. It was the result of a process that began almost as soon as the Organization of American States was established and which had proceeded at an accelerated pace with the passage of time.

It would be unfair to place the blame for this state of affairs entirely on the regional organization, for it is only one segment of the international relations of the American Republics and is no better and no worse than the member governments are prepared to make it. But it does reflect the over-all situation, and if the Organization receives or takes credit when relations are good, it must be prepared to accept part of the blame when they are bad. Nor would it be accurate to say that the Organization has accomplished nothing. In certain fringe areas it can point to progress and to positive achievements. But in many of the basic areas in which it has undertaken to operate not only has the OAS failed to find solutions but in many instances the situation has worsened rather than improved. The spirit of continental unity and solidarity is weaker today than at any time in several decades; basic political differences continue to divide many of the member states; economic and social problems are as far from solution today as ever before.

An appreciation of the current state of inter-American relations and the status of the Organization of American States can perhaps best be gained by an inquiry into the practical measures that have been taken in two important areas of activity, that of peace and security and that of economic and social relations.

Problems of Peace and Security

During the past twelve years the principles and the mechanism of peace and security so laboriously built up in the decade and a half preceding 1948 have been put to a severe test. As described in the preceding chapter, these are embodied in the American Treaty on Pacific Settlement (Pact of Bogotá) and the Inter-American Treaty of Reciprocal Assistance, as well as in the statutes of the Inter-American Peace Committee.

Since 1948 the Organ of Consultation under the Rio de Janeiro Treaty of Reciprocal Assistance has been convoked to deal with no less than eight situations that threatened the peace and security of the Continent. Scarcely had the treaty obtained the minimum number of ratifications to make it operative than it was invoked for the first time to consider the complaint of Costa Rica against Nicaragua in 1948-49. This was followed by the situation in the Caribbean in 1950-51; that of Guatemala in 1954; a second Costa Rican-Nicaraguan controversy in 1955; the case of Honduras and Nicaragua in 1957-58; those of Panama and of Nicaragua in 1959, and finally that of Venezuela against the Dominican Republic in 1960.

During the decade 1950-1960 the Inter-American Peace Committee likewise was active in a number of cases, including those between the Dominican Republic and Cuba in 1948, 1951 and 1956; that of Haiti and the Dominican Republic in 1949; the situation in the Caribbean in 1949; and that between Guatemala, Honduras and Nicaragua in 1954.

It is not the intention of this survey to analyze each of these problems in detail, although that is a project not without interest and one that might well be undertaken by students of inter-American relations. Parenthetically it might be observed that, examined independently, the intervention of the appropriate organ of the Organization in each case was a success. On the surface at least and according to the record, the issue was settled. But examined in their totality it would not be too much to say that nothing was solved. Every one of the foregoing situations involved countries in the Caribbean area, and their settlement was expected to relieve international tensions in that part of the world. But the Caribbean tensions far from being alleviated tended to become worse, culminating in the deplorable case of Venezuela against the Dominican Republic in 1960 and the Cuban Revolution of 1959 with its ramifications in every part of the Continent.

Rather is it desired to inquire into the methods and procedures that were applied in these cases and their possible effect on the future development of the inter-American regional organziation.

In the eight incidents mentioned above in which the Inter-American Treaty of Reciprocal Assistance was invoked, this action was taken on the premise that an aggression had been committed, or that there existed a threat of aggression that jeopardized the peace of the Continent. But every one of the cases with the exception of the last, was settled not by determining the aggressor or by the application of sanctions, but by a process of negotiation and conciliation that is more appropriate to the Treaty on Pacific Settlement than to the Treaty of Reciprocal Assistance.

The question inevitably arises as to why these differences were not submitted to the procedures set forth in the Bogotá Treaty on Pacific Settlement instead of those embodied in the Rio Treaty of Reciprocal Assistance. The answer is that there does not yet exist a continental system of pacific settlement, that the Organization of American States is still operating with an imperfect mechanism in this very important area. Notwithstanding the lapse of twelve years since the Treaty on Pacific Settlement was signed, it has been ratified by only nine governments. It is, then, only half a pact. Because of this defect it has been necessary to resort to improvisation; to lay aside or to ignore what was supposed to be one of the key instruments of the Organization (the Pact of Bogotá) and to use another key instrument (the Rio Treaty) whose primary purpose is entirely different.

It is unfortunate that, despite the efforts of seventy years, the American Republics have not yet been able to conclude a generally acceptable, comprehensive treaty of pacific settlement. The failure not only emphasizes the difficulty of the problem, but the attempts that have been made reflect the tendency that frequently marks the action of Pan American assemblies of trying to go too far too fast. Conference delegates, in the enthusiasm of the moment, incorporate into agreements provisions which the governments later are unwilling to accept, with the result that treaties remain unratified. From the moment of signature at Bogotá in 1948, and considering the number of reservations attached to the treaty at that time, it was a foregone conclusion that this would be the fate of the Pact of Bogotá.

There are undoubted advantages in using the Rio Treaty as a two-fold instrument of pacific settlement and to resist aggression. But as the history of the last twelve years has shown, there are also disadvantages and long-range dangers.

Among the advantages there is the fact that the treaty has been ratified by all twenty-one governments and thus is of continental applicability. Furthermore, every international difference may develop to a point where it threatens the peace and every threat to the peace may jeopardize the sovereignty, independence and territorial integrity of a country, thus calling for the determination of the aggressor and the imposition of sanctions. In addition, the Rio Treaty embodies in Article Six provisions that, by interpretation at least, lend themselves to the procedures of pacific settlement and thus justifies recourse to the treaty for such purposes. And finally, the mechanism of the Rio Treaty is much easier to put into motion than is that of the Treaty on Pacific Settlement, even if the latter were in full effect, which it is not.

Despite the ease and obvious advantages, it is doubtful whether the best interests of the OAS and of the inter-American community have been served by broadening the scope of the Rio Treaty and using it for other than its primary purposes. It was certainly not intended that it should be made to serve in such a manner. In the treaty itself the American States expressed their intention to conclude an Inter-American Peace Treaty to improve the procedures for the pacific settlement of controversies. The Charter of the Organization likewise stipulates that a special treaty will establish adequate procedures for the pacific settlement of disputes and will determine the appropriate means of their application, so that no dispute between American States shall fail of definitive settlement within a reasonable period. In other words the basic instruments of the inter-American regional system were intended to be the Charter of the Organization, the Treaty of Reciprocal Assistance and the Treaty on Pacific Settlement.

The Rio Treaty is primarily a mutual defense pact and it evolved from agreements that originally were directed at aggression from outside the Continent. It was only at Chapultepec in 1945 that the principle that an attack against one American State shall be considered as an attack against all was extended so as to include attacks coming from American as well as non-American states. At Rio de Janeiro in 1947 there was considerable discussion as to whether these two aspects of the problem—the inter- and the intra-continental—should not be separated and treated in distinct agreements.

It is unfortunate that the two features were combined. In some respects the idea of aggression in the Western Hemisphere and the need of making provision for such a contingency, constituted a backward step in the evolution of inter-American relations. It is in conflict with the fundamental premise on which the Pan American system rests; a system that emphasizes the community concept of international relations; that recognizes that international differences may arise but that, when they do, assumes that they shall be settled by the orderly processes of mediation, conciliation or arbitration rather than by force or the imposition of sanctions. That this view continues to predominate is revealed in the approach of the inter-American community to controversies among the member states; it is almost instinctive for the other members to seek to conciliate rather than to place the blame and impose sanctions.

The evolution of the principles of the Rio Treaty parallels in some respects that of the Monroe Doctrine. Both, in their inception, were directed against extra-continental dangers; both, in their successive changes, had their scope extended and their emphasis changed. In the same way that the popularity and the wide public support of the Monroe Doctrine caused its original principles to be changed and diverted to other uses, so also has there been a temptation to use the Rio Treaty for other than its original and primary purposes. Perhaps, as in the case of the Monroe Doctrine, it may some day be considered advisable that the Rio Treaty should in practice be reserved as an instrument to meet threats of aggression from other Continents and that other media be used for purely inter-American problems.

The excessive use of the Rio Treaty in strict inter-American cases and for purposes not within its immediate purview, may in time weaken its effectiveness in any real test to which it may be put should the sovereignty, the independence or the territorial integrity of an American State be jeopardized by an extra-continental threat.

No less disturbing in its potential danger is the tendency that has recently manifested itself of permitting expediency rather than principle to govern the application and operation of the Treaty. In the instances in which it was sought to invoke the Treaty during 1959 and in the one case in which it was applied in 1960, innovations were introduced which, it is feared, were inspired more by considerations of convenience than of conviction.

In accordance with long established practice the Treaty has always been invoked when one country considered that its territorial integrity, sovereignty or political independence were being threatened by another country. In short, it was intended to be applied on behalf of that country which considered itself aggrieved and against another presumed to be the aggressor. But in the 1959 cases of both Panama and Nicaragua the country against which action was sought was not mentioned either in the request for or in the resolution convoking the Organ of Consultation, merely because it was not considered politically expedient to mention Cuba, a government which at the time was enjoying wide popular support throughout the Continent. A few months later the Council of the Organization summarily rejected the request of the Dominican Republic for a meeting of consultation to consider the threat of invasion from Cuba and Venezuela, this time, however, for the opposite political reason that the request had come from a government highly unpopular throughout the Continent and because the request was directed against two governments which at the time were enjoying wide popularity.

None of these cases was, in itself, of great significance, but they all represented a departure from tradition. They raise a question as to whether the Inter-American Treaty of Reciprocal Assistance is to be applied in accordance with juridical principles and well-established precedent, or on the basis of the political atmosphere that may prevail at the moment.

The most recent case to arise under the Rio Treaty, and incidentally the first in which the Organ of Consultation was composed of the Foreign Ministers themselves, was that of Venezuela against the Dom-

inican Republic, arising out of the implication of the latter in the
plot on the life of Venezuela's President. The decision of the Organ of
Consultation was to condemn the action of the Dominican Government, to agree to break off diplomatic relations, and to impose sanctions beginning with the immediate suspension of trade in arms and
implements of war.

Here again the question arises as to whether the Rio Treaty was
applied on the basis of principle or politics. The situation in the
Dominican Republic may be deplorable and the conduct of its
responsible leaders may merit the most severe condemnation. Without
questioning the justness of the decision, the doubt still remains as to
whether this was an appropriate case to come before the Organ of
Consultation under the Inter-American Treaty of Reciprocal Assistance. The primary purpose of the Treaty is to *prevent* aggression,
not to *punish* aggression after it has been committed. The Organ of
Consultation is not a court of justice, nor is the Rio Treaty an instrument to mete out punishment for a crime. Certainly it was not
the intention of the framers of the Rio Treaty that it should be the
medium to bring democracy to a people living under a dictatorial
regime.

The Organization of American States is an inter-governmental institution and as a political entity inevitably it is influenced by political considerations. But it should always be borne in mind that political expediency, carried too far, may undermine the very institution it is expected to uphold. The Rio Treaty is one of the pillars
of the Pan American system. It is important that it remain so, not
only for what it can do in hemisphere relations, but particularly for
what it may be called upon to do in inter-continental relations. As one
reviews events of the past two years, it is difficult to avoid a
feeling of misgiving at a trend which, if permitted to continue, might
have serious consequences on the future effectiveness of this very important instrument. It is to be earnestly hoped that in future applications of the Rio Treaty this trend will be reversed; that it will be
applied in accordance with juridical principles and long-established
procedures; and also that positive measures will be taken to strengthen
other features of the inter-American system to deal with purely inter-
American problems.

At the same time that the Treaty of Rio has thus been weakened,
the effectiveness of the Inter-American Peace Committee has also been
lessened by changes in its scope and methods of operation. From the
date of its organization in 1948, and until 1954, the Committee did

effective work, due largely to the simplicity of its organization and the informality of its procedures. As originally constituted the Committee could begin to function at the request of either party or of any government, and it was also possessed of a considerable degree of initiative in making suggestions and proposing formulas.

Under new statutes drawn up in 1956 pursuant to a resolution of the Tenth Inter-American Conference, the value of the Committee has been largely nullified. Only if both parties wish to avail themselves of its services may the Committee begin to function, and then only in accordance with the methods and procedures agreed upon by the parties. The Committee is now surrounded by all the procedural formalities that have made the conventional agreements on pacific settlement so ineffective. It is not surprising that following the adoption of the new statutes and until 1959, the Peace Committee held only one meeting each year, to welcome the new and to bid farewell to the outgoing Chairman. Although in the latter year, at the Fifth Meeting of Consultation of American Foreign Ministers, the Committee was given some temporary additional authority in relation to the then existing tensions in the Caribbean, this action did not broaden its basic authority and its intervention was limited to the collection and publication of factual information.

On balance, then, and in the light of developments of the past two years, the OAS is weaker today in the field of peace and security than at any time in its twelve year history.

Economic and Social Factors

In the political area of peace and security there is at least a surface appearance of accomplishment between 1948 and 1960. In contrast, in the economic and social the surface has barely been scratched. This despite the fact that since 1948 the dominant world issue has been economic. It is the one theme that has commanded national as well as international concern, among the member states of the inter-American as well as the world organization. In the Western Hemisphere it is the one problem of continental import. The essentially political issues have largely revolved around a limited number of states in the Caribbean; the economic and social problems concern every government and affect every people.

At Bogotá in 1948 it was agreed that a special inter-American conference should be held at Buenos Aires during the last quarter of 1948 or no later than the first quarter of 1949, to take decisions on economic problems affecting the nations of the Western Hemisphere. The conference finally met in the second half of 1957. This delay is not to be attributed to indifference, certainly not on the part of the vast majority of the American States. Neither does it mean that economic problems received no attention during these years. On the contrary, the Inter-American Economic and Social Council, the principal agency under the Bogotá Charter operating in the economic and social field, has been in almost continuous session throughout these twelve years. In 1956, following the meeting in Panama of the Chiefs of State of the American Republics, a Committee of Presidential Representatives was appointed composed of personal envoys of the heads of government. And finally, at the end of 1958, a Special Committee to Study the Formulation of New Measures for Economic Cooperation, a title, understandably enough, popularly shortened to Committee of Twenty-one, was named. Both of these two last mentioned bodies had as their primary purpose the formulation of an inter-American program that would contribute to the solution of the economic and social problems of the member states.

If the time devoted and the agencies involved were the test of accomplishment, the achievements of the OAS in the economic and social field would be overwhelming. That greater progress has not been made reflects the difficulty of the problem and the seriousness of the differences that have developed as to how it can best be solved.

It would be a mistake to assume that no economic progress has been made in the Western Hemisphere during the past twelve years. Some countries have experienced considerable growth in trade, in investment, in industry; but this growth has taken place in spite of rather than because of the inter-American regional organization. It is precisely in the area of inter-governmental action, and inter-governmental action on the multilateral level in which the Organization operates, that after twelve years of effort very little progress has been made in advancing the economic and social welfare of the community of American States. Even where progress has been made the rate of growth has not kept pace with the population increase.

The economic issues have revolved principally around the stabilization of existing economies, and the strengthening of national economies through further development and diversification, including industrialization. Closely related to these essentially economic objectives are the social implications of economic development.

Lack of housing, insufficient schools, inadequate public health and sanitation facilities, of transportation and communications, and other elements that contribute to the national progress of a people have confronted every Latin American country throughout history. A growing awareness of these deficiencies is at the bottom of the social unrest that has characterized the national life of Latin America in the years since the close of World War II.

The political issues that today confront so many nations of the Continent, including the danger of communism and the threat to the democratic concept of government, are largely an outgrowth of these basic problems, and the failure to make any appreciable progress in their solution.

The combination of these two objectives—economic development and social betterment—has created for the inter-American regional organization problems greater than any it has faced since the decade of the twenties. At that time it was confronted with another crisis growing out of the practice of unilateral intervention by the United Sates in the affairs of other countries. The failure of the Organization thus far to deal adequately with current problems explains the decline and deterioration that has marked the recent history of inter-American relations.

Given the nature of the problem and the relative stages of development of the member states, the consideration of the issues within the framework of the inter-American regional organization almost invariably has involved a grouping of the Latin American countries on the one hand and the United States on the other; so much so that at times it has appeared that the OAS has ceased to be the Organization of American States and has become the Organization of Latin America versus the United States. The circumstance that the United States held the key to the problems inevitably had its repercussions in the over-all relations of the United States and Latin America, and on the ability of the Organization to cope with them.

During much of the period under review the attitude of the United States has been marked by two characteristics: One, an unwillingness, at least in the Latin American view, to do as much as needed to be done; and, secondly, when it was prepared to act at all, in a preference to act not through the multilateral facilities of the inter-American regional system but on a bilateral country-by-country basis. On both counts the regional organization labored under handicaps. On the first, because its efforts proved futile and it merely dissipated its time in useless discussion; on the second, when it might have done something constructive it was denied the opportunity because of a preference for other means.

The United States preference for the bilateral treatment of economic problems was reiterated as recently as March, 1960, by President Eisenhower when in his report to the nation following his South American trip he made the statement: "While certain problems are continental in scope, nonetheless each of the countries I visited — indeed, each of the twenty republics of Latin America — is highly individual. Each has its own unique problems and ideas regarding future development. Hence, our cooperation with each republic must be tailored to its particular situation."

There is logic in this point of view, but if carried too far it may adversely affect the hemisphere organization. In the interest of strengthening this feature of inter-American relations a special effort must be made to have those problems that are "continental in scope" handled through the multilateral facilities of the regional system.

Commodity Stabilization

Price and market stabilization of basic commodities has been one of the key problems in inter-American economic discussions during the past twelve years. For the countries of Latin America there is nothing more important and, up to the present, more difficult of attainment. To them it is an essential factor in preserving the soundness of their existing economies, and a prelude to further steps that may be taken toward economic development and diversification.

Instability in world markets and prices for their basic commodities has been a chronic problem for Latin America, arising out of the nature of its economy and the narrow foundations on which it rests. Traditionally these countries have been producers of raw materials, agricultural and mineral, which they themselves do not consume to any great extent, and which they ship to other countries in exchange for the manufactured goods which they do not produce. Theirs is essentially an export economy, revolving around two or three and sometimes only a single commodity; and their ability to market these products frequently depends not on what they themselves do, but on what other countries may do and on the policies and practices which those countries may adopt. Their economic well-being is dependent to an extraordinary degree on world markets and prices, and on forces over which they have little or no control. Invariably raw materials are the first to feel the effects of changing market conditions, and the fluctuations in the prices of and in the demand for these commodities are usually the most extreme and the most abrupt.

Latin America has long sought to protect itself against these violent fluctuations, but the problem, despite its obvious importance, is extremely difficult to solve. Unilateral action by individual countries will not succeed, for rarely does a nation have such a complete monopoly of a commodity. The nearest approach to such an enviable national position was that of Chile and natural nitrate between 1880 and 1920. Most commodities, whether agricultural or mineral, are produced in several countries and any attempt on the part of one to influence markets and prices merely stimulates production in others, as Brazil found to its sorrow with its several attempts at the valorization of coffee.

Coffee is an outstanding example, not only of the problem's importance but of the difficulty of finding an adequate solution. Grown in fifteen Latin American countries, it is the principal money crop and the source of the economic well being of many of these countries. Brazil depends upon its coffee exports for sixty per cent of its foreign exchange, Colombia and El Salvador for about eighty per cent. It has been estimated that a drop of only one cent per pound in the price of coffee represents for Brazil a foreign exchange loss of $19,000,-000 a year; for Colombia, $10,000,000 and for the Central American Republics, $7,000,000. In 1960 it was estimated that Latin America's income from the foreign sale of coffee was $1,000,000,000 less than it had been a few years earlier. In the light of these figures economic assistance and international loans mean little when they do not even offset the losses from the normal operations of international trade and finance.

Inevitably the problem was injected into the councils of the inter-American regional organization. In the Latin American view, a Pan American coffee agreement, to be really effective, should include not only the Latin American producers but also the United States as the world's principal consumer; they also felt that such a pact should establish import quotas into the United States, thus assuring to the Western Hemisphere producers a fixed share of this great consuming market. Far from becoming a party to such an agreement, the United States long refused even to participate in the discussion of it on the ground that artificial measures of this nature were contrary to sound economic principles and, in any event, that it was a matter for the producing countries to solve.

It was only after the visit of Vice President Nixon to South America in 1958, and due it is feared more to his unpleasant experiences than to any change in convictions, that the United States undertook a more active role. In 1958 an international coffee commission meeting in Washington worked out an agreement among the Latin American producers fixing export quotas for the next crop year. This was a palliative but hardly a solution, for it merely placed limitations on Latin American participation in world markets without corresponding limitations on other producing countries. The long-range effect of such an agreement would have been merely to stimulate coffee growing in low cost producing countries at the expense of Latin America. The following year, in 1959, a further step was taken in the negotiation of a general international coffee agreement fixing export quotas for both Latin American and African producers. In both these negotiations the United States, although not a party to either agreement, participated and used its good offices to facilitate an understanding.

Both of these arrangements were better than no agreement at all. But the question still remains whether they constitute a real solution; whether adequate measures have yet been taken to adjust production to demand; and whether, if production is not more closely geared to consumption, it is possible to stabilize prices merely by allocating export quotas. The 1959 agreement has reasonably stabilized coffee prices. In the Latin American view, they could not have gone much lower. In the Latin American view, also, more needs to be done to place the coffee industry on a reasonably firm and stable basis.

International Consequences of National Economic Policies

Closely related to the delays and failures in negotiating fully satisfactory commodity agreements are the international repercussions that not infrequently flow from national decisions designed to protect domestic commodity prices and markets. During the past decade there have been several such instances involving the United States on the one hand and the other American Republics on the other. They pose the question as to what if any, obligation, a nation has, in fixing its national economic policies, to take into consideration the effect on the economies of other countries. To what extent should the United States, in adopting measures of this nature, be influenced by the effect, for instance on Uruguay, of limitations on the importation of wool; on Mexico, Peru and Bolivia, of import quotas on lead and zinc; on Venezuela, in the case of petroleum. And further, when and through what media, if at all, should these countries have an opportunity to express their views on such proposed measures?

These are all concrete cases that have occurred in recent years. In each instance the measures were intended to protect declining activities in the United States. Examined strictly from the national point of view, they were reasonable and justifiable. But for the Latin American producers of the same commodities, whose economies already operate on too narrow a base, who may have seen the world demand and the world prices for these commodities decline as much as fifty per cent within twelve months, the prospect of a further curtailment of the opportunity to market their already reduced output conjures up possibilities of economic disaster.

In addition to their economic consequences, the political effect of such measures may be far-reaching, as was indicated in the case of Chile, when the mere suggestion in 1958 of a higher import duty on copper, on which that country depends for sixty per cent of its foreign exchange, resulted in the abrupt cancellation of a protocolary visit to the United States that had already been scheduled for the Chilean President. Similarly, the announcement of the lead and zinc quotas that same year, reducing by thirty per cent the imports of these commodities from Mexico, Peru and Bolivia — an announcement made, curiously, on the eve of a meeting in Washington of the Foreign Ministers of the American Republics to consider the means of improving inter-American economic relations — resulted in a resolution by the Congress of Peru for the immediate withdrawal of the Peruvian Foreign Minister from the Washington meeting.

Inevitably measures of this nature engender ill-will. They affect not only the relations of the countries immediately concerned, but their repercussions extend throughout the whole regional organization. They also arouse a determination, quite understandable, to deal with other countries that are prepared to trade in these commodities, whatever the political consequences. For the countries affected, there is sometimes involved not merely a matter of dollars and cents, but a problem of economic survival.

Obviously, these are situations that do not lend themselves to easy solution. Every government must be expected to take the measures it considers to be in the best interest of its nationals. Nor is it likely that any government would submit to the approval or disapproval of any other state or states measures of this nature which it deems necessary.

At the same time the twenty-one American Republics are members of the inter-American community and, as such, have assumed obligations toward one another. They have subscribed to certain basic principles that govern their mutual relations: the principle of cooperation and reciprocal aid in the solution of common problems; the principle that the welfare of each is dependent upon the welfare of all; and that what affects one member of the community inevitably has its repercussions on all the others. An ability to work out a formula to deal with such issues is a test of the effectiveness of the inter-American regional system.

Economic and Social Development

Paralleling the emphasis on stabilization of commodity prices and markets has been the attempt to find a satisfactory formula to promote the economic development of the less advanced areas of the Continent. The two problems — dependence on a few key commodities and a broadening of the economic base—are interrelated. To the extent that the countries of Latin America are able to stimulate their economic growth, to develop industries, to convert into finished goods a larger proportion of the raw materials they now export, to that extent will they relieve themselves of their present dependence on a few basic commodities.

The Latin American economy needs to be developed at a much faster rate than it is now progressing. These nations do not have the resources to do this themselves, but must look to outside sources to satisfy their capital requirements. Throughout the period under review there has been general agreement on the objective; its realization has been impeded by a difference of philosophy and practice between the United States on the one hand and virtually all of Latin America on the other. This difference revolves largely around the use of private versus public funds, the adequacy or inadequacy of existing credit institutions, the channels through which additional funds should be made available, and the extent of official participation in economic activities.

Capital for industrial development has come and undoubtedly will continue to come largely from private sources. Huge sums have already gone to Latin America, as reflected in the more than eight billion dollars of United States capital invested throughout the Continent. Although much of this has gone into the extractive industries, no inconsiderable amount has contributed to the industrial development that has taken place in many sections of the Continent in recent years.

But there are many activities that do not lend themselves to private financing and that can only be undertaken through public funds and public agencies. Here the first difference of opinion has arisen. On the one hand, Latin American sentiment favors a broadening of the area of state participation in economic development, either through the medium of public funds or, if private capital is to be used, that it be invested through state institutions. Sentiment of the United States on the other hand, favors a narrowing of the area reserved for state action, leaving a much wider field for private capital and initiative.

However wide or narrow the zone appropriate for private enterprise may finally become, there will always be an area that does not attract private capital and in which, if anything is to be done, it must be done through state agencies and with public funds. Examples of such activities are transportation, particularly highways; power development, irrigation and reclamation projects, and certain types of social services such as housing, land utilization, educational, public health and sanitation projects.

On the need of public intervention in such activities there is general agreement. But from 1948 to 1958 a difference of opinion existed with respect to the adequacy and the type of institution through which funds should be made available.

The International Bank for Reconstruction and Development and the International Monetary Fund, as well as national agencies of the United States, such as the Export-Import Bank, the International Cooperation Administration and the Development Loan Fund, have long operated in Latin America as in other parts of the world. Despite the aid afforded by these institutions, the opinion long prevailed in Latin America that their facilities were inadequate; that their policies were oriented more in the direction of other parts of the world than toward Latin America. Not a little resentment was aroused among Latin Americans when they were denied participation in the Marshall Plan or some comparable arrangement, and the feeling has also existed that because they are farther removed from the immediate threat of communist imperialism, they have received only a fraction of the economic assistance accorded other countries.

For many years proposals had been advanced for the establishment of a bank or development institution that would be strictly inter-American in its organization and administration and which, it was believed, would be better equipped to satisfy the needs of the American Republics. In fact, the idea of a Pan American bank is as old as the Pan American movement itself, but for decades it never progressed beyond the talking stage. Although supported in early years by the United States, none of the more recent proposals prospered principally because of lack of United States support, which consistently contended that existing credit facilities were adequate and additional institutions, international or regional, were not needed.

Not until 1958, and again it is feared the decision was born of expediency following the South American visit of Vice President Nixon rather than conviction that, with the support of the United States were steps taken toward the creation of an Inter-American Development ment Bank. Capitalized at $1,000,000,000, of which $850,000,000 represents authorized capital stock that will be available for ordinary banking operations and a special fund of $150,000,000 for projects that would not be able to meet the usual banking requirements for a loan, the bank began to function in 1960.

The psychological effect of the establishment of the bank has been favorable. Its practical value must await the test of time.

Financing is only one aspect of economic development. The Inter-American Development Bank is in no sense a complete answer to the problem but it does represent the first collective step taken by all except one of the member states [Cuba] of the inter-American regional organization to seek a partial solution and to make a combined contribution to at least one important feature of economic development.

Basic to the total problem of economic development is a plan or program of action, and although this has been the subject of interminable discussion within the Inter-American Economic and Social Council, the specialized conferences and numerous committees, no comprehensive continental program has yet been devised setting forth in precise terms what collective measures should be taken and how they should be carried out. This failure may also be attributed to the difference of philosophy and practice between the United States on the one hand and the Latin American countries on the other, a difference that has characterized so much of the economic discussion of the last twelve years.

Economic activity and economic cooperation there have been, of course, even within the framework of the inter-American regional organization. The program of technical cooperation sponsored by the Inter-American Economic and Social Council and the technical activities of the several specialized organizations have had economic development and social improvement as their major objective. Nor have they not been without some effect. But taken in the aggregate these have been minor operations, producing scarcely a ripple in the vast sea of economic and social need. In recent years even these activities have tended to lose their impact in the maze of discussion and the general frustration that has marked the economic and social endeavors of the Organization.

The nearest approach to a collective program of economic cooperation is the so-called Operation Pan America, based upon the proposal made by President Juscelino Kubitschek of Brazil in 1958. From the standpoint of the inter-American regional organization the great virtue of this proposal is the spirit that inspired it and the continental concept on which it is based. When the Brazilian President first advanced his idea in a letter to President Eisenhower he suggested the need of "a thorough revision of policy" and "a comprehensive reappraisal of Pan American ideals in all their aspects and implications." As he further defined it: "Operation Pan America is not an undertaking limited by time, with objectives to be attained in a short period; rather is it a reorientation of hemisphere policy, intended to place Latin America, by a process of full appraisement, in a position to participate more effectively in the defense of the West . . . Operation Pan America is more than a mere program; it is an entire policy." Applied in this spirit, its psychological possibilities were invaluable. Properly used, it could have served as a rallying point to unite the twenty-one nations in acting collectively to meet the one great issue that today confronts the nations of the Western Hemisphere.

Operation Pan America has suffered from the defect of imprecision. It has tended to emphasize ends without a clear enunciation of the means by which they were to be attained. Its primary objective has been to raise the standard of living of the Latin American population by an intensive and extensive program of economic development.

Perhaps this lack of precision in its practical aspects explains the lukewarmness, not to say indifference, with which operation Pan America was received and the slowness it has experienced in becoming a working reality. But the objective has always had an appeal, especially in Latin America. This, coupled with Brazilian persistence, has kept Operation Pan America an active subject of discussion in the councils of the Organization. It received what is perhaps its strongest official endorsement in the Act of Bogotá drawn up in September of 1960 by the Special Committee of Twenty-one, in which it was declared that the economic development of Latin America requires prompt action "within the framework of Operation Pan America." The Act further recognizes the need of long-term lending to promote economic development and of cooperative action to stabilize the exchange earnings of countries heavily dependent upon the exportation of primary products.

The Act of Bogotá is likewise significant for the formal recognition it gives to the social implications of economic development and the need of positive action to promote the social betterment of the under-privileged masses. This also has been the subject of prolonged debate, but no comprehensive program of inter-American action has ever been worked out. The Act of Bogotá sets forth in elaborate detail measures for social improvements in the conditions of rural living and land use, of housing and community facilities, of public health, and of educational systems and training facilities. As in the case of the proposals for economic development, it contemplates that these shall be undertaken "within the framework of Operation Pan America."

Both in its economic development and social betterment features the Act of Bogotá is merely a series of recommendations. It is true they have been made an untold number of times in the past. But here they are couched in stronger terms and in their formulation it is possible to discern a change in the attitude of the member governments, a growing awareness of the nature of the problem, and a disposition to take collective action to meet it. The one positive feature of the plan is the $500,000,000 offer of the United States, appropriation of which has been authorized by Congress, to constitute a special fund for social development and to be administered by the Inter-American Development Bank.

However, the conditional nature of the program is reflected in the paragraph of the Act of Bogotá which reads: "It is understood that the purpose of the special fund would be to contribute capital resources and technical assistance on flexible terms and conditions, including repayment in local currency and the relending of repaid funds, in accordance with appropriate and selective criteria in the light of the resources available, to support the efforts of the Latin American countries that are prepared to initiate or expand effective institutional improvements and to adopt measures to employ efficiently their own resources with a view to achieving greater social progress and more balanced economic growth."

The Act of Bogotá is not a program ready for immediate implementa-

tion. Rather it is a blueprint for future action, drawn perhaps in hues
a little rosier than others, but still only a blueprint. As such it is a
challenge to the member states that each should do its part, and to the
agencies of the Organization to demonstrate a capacity for the effective implementation of the program.

CHAPTER VI

THE OAS TODAY

The great need of the OAS today is leadership, guidance and direction. These qualities have always been necessary, but now more so than ever if the inter-American regional organization is to meet the challenge that confronts it.

The OAS needs to reappraise its basic policies and objectives. It must determine what the purposes of the Organization are, what it can and cannot do, what is appropriate and what is inappropriate for an inter-governmental institution to undertake.

The Organization must realize, as must also the member governments and the people of the several countries, that the regional organization is not the sum total of international relations in the Western Hemisphere. It is only a part, in fact a very small part, and a distinction must be made between those things that come within its sphere of action and those that must be reserved for other media of international negotiation.

Equally important is the distinction that must be recognized between international and national issues. The principle of non-intervention is so firmly established that it hardly requires further discussion; yet there are times when the Organization itself tends to overstep its bounds and to engage in activities beyond its capacity to fulfill.

The Charter of the Organization embodies numerous principles, norms and standards intended to govern the national and the international life of its members. The ability to distinguish between rights and obligations that are international in character and thus appropriate for action within the framework of the inter-American regional organization, and hopes to which a people may aspire but which they must seek through their own national channels and institutions, constitutes a test of the wisdom and statesmanship of the responsible leaders of the Organization.

During 1960 the Council of the Organization engaged in a prolonged debate on the creation of an Inter-American Commission on Human Rights. As originally conceived and as submitted to the governments for approval, the statutes would have authorized the Commission to entertain appeals from any person or group of persons who felt that

they had suffered a denial of justice in their respective countries and
to propose the corrective measures that should be taken. There is
much to be done to promote respect for human rights in every American
country and in this area the Organization can do effective work. But
the time has not yet come for the creation of a court or commission
that would come between a government and its nationals. International organization in the Western Hemisphere has not yet progressed
to such a point. Fortunately, as finally aproved, the authority of the
Commission is limited to the promotional aspect of the problem. Notwithstanding, the Commission, in its first report, insisted that "if
it is to fulfill its high mission to the people of America" its duties
must not be limited merely to promoting respect for human rights,
but it must be authorized to see that these rights are not violated. It
accordingly requested a modification of its statues. Such is the lack
of reality that today characterizes much of the functioning of the
OAS.

No less unrealistic are efforts to bring to a people the blessings of
democracy by the imposition of sanctions. Here the Organization is
treading on even more dangerous ground, for the issue has gone beyond
the stage of theoretical debate and has found expression in an actual
attempt to oust the existing regime in the Dominican Republic. However desirable it may be to replace dictatorship with democracy, it is
difficult to avoid the conclusion that in the 1960 case of Venezuela
versus the Dominican Republic the Council of the Organization and
the Meeting of Foreign Ministers sacrificed principle to expediency;
that in response to pressure and popular demand the Rio Treaty of
Reciprocal Assistance was used to punish rather than to restrain,
and that sanctions were imposed for national rather than international
purposes. This is hardly the way to build an institution on firm
and durable foundations. Not only is it an abuse of one of the basic
instruments of the inter-American system, but the OAS has undertaken
a responsibility that it is unable to fulfill. Once the dictatorship of
Trujillo has come to an end, can the OAS assure that democracy will
automatically follow in the Dominican Republic? What advantage,
it might be asked, would there be either for the Dominican people or
for the inter-American community to get rid of Trujillo only to have
him replaced by a Castro? It has well been observed, and the responsible agencies of the OAS should bear the observation in mind that
"Democracy does not spread from one republic to its neighbors like
a disease or a fashion in wall paper. Where it appears at all, it grows

from roots which can take hold of something tangible in the social situation and draw nourishment from its surroundings."

There is much that the inter-American regional organization can do; there are many things that it cannot do. No less important than to know what it can and should do is to recognize its limitations. To paraphrase the admonition of Lord Bryce in his study of *Modern Democracies,* do not give to an international institution powers for which it is unripe, in the simple faith that the tool will give skill to the workman's hand. After all, international organization is a relatively recent innovation, scarcely known a half century ago, and not fully understood even today. It would be unfortunate if, through an excess of zeal, it should undertake responsibilities for which it is not yet prepared and which could only result, as Joaquim Nabuco expressed it a half century ago, in "killing at its inception an institution which is worthy of enduring throughout the centuries."

Even more important to the future of the OAS than this tendency to engage in activities beyond its capacity are several trends that have recently appeared in the area of inter-American relations; trends which, if permitted to develop, may in time undermine and destroy the Organization as a continental institution.

The virtual eviction of the Dominican Republic and the withdrawal of Cuba from the inter-American regional system during 1960 can only be viewed with dismay. It is distressing because it is contrary to the basic concept on which the Pan American movement was founded and on which it has evolved. Whatever justification there may have been for the one, and however unavoidable the other, the two cases represent a profound weakening of the structure of the Organization. They reflect the essentially negative character of inter-American relations during the past twelve years. Prevention of discord and concilition of differences obviously have a place in international relations; but this alone is not enough. The strength of the inter-American system lies in its positive approach to hemispheric problems; the formulation of programs of affirmative action designed to promote the welfare and thus contribute to the unity and solidarity of the member states.

To what extent, it might be asked, has the Organization contributed to the stresses and strains that today confront it? If a broad continental program of economic and social cooperation had been initiated some ten or twelve years ago, might it have anticipated the demand for social betterment and economic improvement that is today so prevalent throughout the Continent? Might it thereby have avoided the social revolutions with their political, economic and social upheavals and international complications that have marked the recent histories of Guatemala, Bolivia and Cuba, and that threaten to repeat themselves in other countries?

During the past decade the Council of the Organization on at least half a dozen occasions has served as provisional organ of consultation in conflicts between the so-called forces of democracy and of dictatorship in the countries of the Caribbean. In every instance it pursued a course of concilation which merely evaded the basic issue and solved nothing. If it had adopted a firmer stand, if it had had the courage to distinguish between the aggressor and the aggrieved, might it have allayed the tensions and perhaps avoided the unpleasant incident between Venezuela and the Dominican Republic in 1960? By such firm action, might it also have advanced the cause of representative democracy by imposing restraints on the forces of dictatorship?

These rhetorical questions are intended to emphasize that the strength of the inter-American system lies in its positive approach to hemisphere problems; in the adoption of affimative programs of economic, social, and cultural cooperation. Only to the extent that it pursues such a course can it hope to preserve the unity and solidarity of its members.

It must be assumed that the cases of Cuba and the Dominican Republic are temporary situations that will be corrected in time. They must be corrected, for if they were to persist and become permanent, the very foundations of the system would be undermined and the entire structure endangered.

No less serious than these immediate problems that have tended to destroy the unity of the Organization is the trend toward the utilization of other media in dealing with inter-American problems than those afforded by the regional organization. This trend is evident particularly in the consideration of economic and social problems, and involves the issue of multilateralism, bilateralism and sub-regionalism. Are the problems that present themselves among the nations of the Western Hemisphere to be solved by bilateral negotiations between individual states, by the creation of sub-regional groupings, or through the multilateral facilities of the OAS?

In the Western Hemisphere neither multilateralism nor bilateralism should or can be used to the exclusion of the other. Inevitably, and this is particularly true in the economic field, most problems must be dealt with on a country-by-country basis. But if the inter-American regional organization is to be preserved, it must be prepared to do its

part in the economic and social no less than in the political area of
inter-American relations. The Organization of American States does
not operate in a series of isolated compartments. It is an integrated
whole, and each part must function if the whole is to work.

The greatest failure of the inter-American regional system since the
Charter of the Organization was signed in 1948 has been its inability
to have basic economic issues considered within the framework of the
Organization. The insistance that economic problems can be dealt
with only on a bilateral, country-by-country basis has had a tremendous psychological effect. Among the Latin American members of
the inter-American community it has aroused mounting dissatisfaction
with the economic policies of the United States; at the same time it
has created an attitude of frustration and futility toward the inter-
American regional system.

In the American Continent the bilateral treatment of economic
questions is in reality a unilateral approach to the problem. Given the
nature of the questions dealt with, their relation to credits, the financing of economic development, and the marketing and prices of basic
commodities, the attitude of the United States is almost decisive. By
insisting on the bilateral approach the United States has in effect set
itself up as the arbiter of what shall be discussed, how the discussions
shall be conducted and, in large measure, the decision that should
be made.

The emphasis on the bilateral approach has developed a form of bilateralism in the Western Hemisphere that has many inherent dangers:
a bilateralism of the United States versus Latin America. There could
be nothing more dangerous for the inter-American regional organization than for a situation to develop whereby one country would find
itself on one side of an issue and all the others on the other side. And
yet, that is exactly what is happening in the economic field, in which
the United States invariably finds itself opposed by every other American republic on every economic issue that presents itself. Such an
alignment is not good, either for the United States or for Latin America, and certainly not for the inter-American regional system. The
effect of this tendency is to undermine the community concept of
inter-American relations, the concept that the problems of the Continent, whether military, political or economic, are not the responsibility of any one nation but the collective responsibility of the community of American States.

An inevitable consequence of this form of bilateralism is the emphasis on sub-regionalism, a feeling that the economic unification of

Latin America is the only way to solve the economic problems of the region. A latent sentiment for Latin American regionalism in contradistinction to Pan Americanism, has always existed and today it is finding tangible expression in the proposal for a Latin American economic union. Strong arguments are being advanced not only in Latin America but by economic thinkers and policy makers in the United States, that integration is the economic salvation of Latin America.

From the standpoint of its potential effect on the continental inter-American system, this proposal merits the closest scrutiny. The acceptance of the argument that the economic problems of Latin America can be solved only through integration is an admission of the bankruptcy of Pan Americanism; a recognition that the economic problems of the member states cannot be solved within the framework of the continental Pan American organization, and that a new economic alignment must be devised to meet them.

It has been well observed that economic integration inevitably implies a degree of political integration; not necessarily in the sense of political union, but certainly political understanding in order to give effect to the objectives of the economic arrangement. Considering the extent to which economics today dominate national life, this could represent a considerable degree of common political action.

The effect of such a development on the existing inter-American regional organization, and on the relationship of the United States to the other member states, would be far-reaching. Instead of being one of twenty-one, the United States would be one — not necessarily against twenty but in no better position in relation to them than any other country or group of countries in any part of the world. What this would eventually do to the Pan American system, to the Organization of American States, is easy to visualize.

No one who is at all familiar with the history of Pan American relations should be prepared to admit that the economic problems of the American Republics cannot be solved with the framework of the hemisphere organization, or at least that it can play a role in this area. There was a time when a similar doubt prevailed with respect to the political problems of the Continent; that peace and security could not be made the collective responsibility of all, but was the unilateral obligation of each. If the delicate and sometimes highly explosive political problem of intervention that existed between the United States on the one side and all Latin America on the other during the first three decades of the century, could be settled by the collective, multilateral approach, it should certainly be possible to find formulas that will enable the twenty-one governments to work together for the solution of their common economic problems.

Operation Pan America, as advocated by President Juscelino Kubitschek of Brazil, reflects that vision and spirit that the present situation calls for. In the United States, this continental concept has found a counterpart in the proposal of Governor Nelson Reckefeller for the creation of a Pan American Economic Union. Ability to meet this test is the challenge that confronts the inter-American regional organization in the decade of the '60s.

Leadership of the Council

The leadership required to meet this challenge, to reverse the dangerous trends that have recently appeared, and to promote a positive program of constructive action, could well come from several sources.

Within the Organization it might most logically be expected from the Council of the Organization. By the terms of the Charter it is the permanent, executive committee of the inter-American system, composed of representatives of ambassadorial rank from each member state, sitting in continuous session and thus in a position not only to exercise general supervision over the affairs of the Organization, but to take prompt action in emergencies. The membership of the Council functions in a two-fold capacity: First, as representatives of individual sovereign states; secondly, as a corporate body to promote the collective welfare and the unity and solidarity of the community of American states.

In its over-all influence the Council is more important than the Inter-American Conference. Although the latter is the supreme organ of the Organization, it is an *ad hoc* body meeting only every five years. The Council, furthermore, has a relationship to every other agency of the Organization. No one is in a better position to evaluate the elements of strength and weakness and to make appropriate recommendations to the governments and to the Inter-American Conference.

The Economic and Social Council, the Cultural Council and the Council of Jurists are dependent organs of the Council of the Organization. The Pan American Union is responsible to it for the proper discharge of its duties. Agreements between the Council and the specialized agencies require them to submit their work programs and budgets and they give to the Council important supervisory authority in matters relating to fiscal and organizational changes. By the

Charter and by specific resolution the Council is authorized to make recommendations to the governments and to the Inter-American Conference on any matter that affects the functioning of the Organization.

And yet the Council has not measured up to its possibilities. This may be due to the caliber of its membership, which is not as high as it might be. As international organization has grown and the demands upon governments for participation in international institutions has increased, it is understandable if at times the caliber of representation should decline. An interesting subject of investigation would be a comparative study of the personalities who at different times comprised the membership of the old Governing Board of the Pan American Union and those who in recent years have served on the Council of the Organization of American States.

However, the failure to measure up may be due, and this is more likely, to intrinsic weaknesses that have developed within the Organization. The principal matters that have come before the Council during the past ten years are those that it has been called upon to consider as the provisional organ of consultation under the Rio Treaty of Reciprocal Assistance. In many respects these have been the sole reason for its existence. Without discounting their importance, these are issues that tend to divide and separate rather than to unite. The debates in the Council have with increasing frequency degenerated into heated, acrimonious and bitter exchanges and hence, the Council has contributed little to the development of that community spirit that is the basic premise on which the Organization rests.

In one of his typically imaginative and visionary speeches, Governor Nelson Rockefeller recently advanced the idea of a confederation of the nations of the Western Hemisphere. Utopian though it may sound, in 1960 it is a long-range possibility that should not be lightly dismissed. It is an objective on which the advocates of Pan Americanism should constantly set their sights. Perhaps in a period of time equal to that which elapsed between the first proposal of an inter-American security pact by Simón Bolívar in 1825 and the actual signing of the Rio Treaty of Reciprocal Assistance in 1947, such a confederation may become a reality. In any event, in its corporate capacity this is the spirit that should inspire the Council of the Organization; a spirit, unfortunately, that has been conspicuously absent during the past decade.

Failure of the Council to play a more positive role in inter-American relations may also be due to an innate lack of confidence on the part of the member governments, an unwillingness to delegate too much authority to the Council because of its physical location in Washington. In this respect, the Council is still laboring under the heritage of the past when the Secretary of State of the United States was *ex officio* Chairman, when the other governments were represented by their diplomatic agents in Washington, and when the absence of diplomatic relations with the United States also meant no representation on the Council. These bases of organization also recall the remark of the Secretary of State who, when the question of a site for the new home of the Pan American Union was under consideration back in 1907, is reported to have remarked that it was immaterial to him where the building was located, so long as it was convenient to the Department of State.

Although this situation has long been a thing of the past, it still hangs like a cloud over the Council. It explains the refusal of the framers of the Charter to delegate to the Council blanket authority to take action "on every matter that affects the . . . solidarity and general welfare of the American Republics." It explains why the authority of the Council was restricted to those matters specifically entrusted to it by the Inter-American Conference or the Meeting of Consultation. It is an attitude reflected in the statement of the Chilean delegate at Bogotá in 1948 that "it is not appropriate that all American activities have their seat in Washington." It also explains why a number of delegations at that time were prepared to modify the Rio de Janeiro Treaty of Reciprocal Assistance in order that the powers of the Council set forth in that treaty might be entrusted to another body. That this sentiment was more than the personal opinion of an individual delegate and reflected a feeling widely held among the member states is confirmed by the action taken at the Tenth Inter-American Conference at Caracas in 1954, reaffirming the decision denying general political authority to the Council.

Inevitably the question is posed: Is there too much concentration of inter-American authority in Washington? If the seat of the Council were to be established elsewhere than in Washington, would there be a disposition on the part of the member governments to delegate to it greater authority, perhaps even that of acting on every matter that affects the solidarity and general welfare of the American Republics? And in that event, would the governments also be inclined to raise the level of their representation, not so much in title as in quality, so that the Council could adequately undertake the responsibilities corresponding to it? If so, the transfer might be worth contemplating.

In addition to the Council, Washington is the seat of the Pan American Union, the general secretariat of the Organization; the Inter-American Economic and Social Council, the Inter-American Defense Board, the Inter-American Development Bank, and the largest of the specialized agencies, the Pan American Health Organization. This represents a considerable concentration of agencies. It is easy to overemphasize physical location of an activity, but its psychological effect should not be discounted. It is not only what is done, but where and how that influences official as well as popular reaction. The desirability of a degree of decentralization is certainly a subject worthy of study, either by the Inter-American Conference or by some other appropriate agency of the Organization.

Leadership of the Secretariat

In achieving the long-range objectives of the OAS and in giving effect to constructive programs of inter-American cooperation, a considerable degree of leadership might be expected to come from the General Secretariat.

The leadership of the Secretariat must of necessity be of a special kind. It is one that guides rather than directs. It derives its influence from the confidence that the Secretariat is able to inspire in the governments and in the representative bodies it is expected to serve. Any pretense on the part of the Secretariat to play other than a subordinate, behind-the-scenes role, any ambition it may have to direct and to dictate, not only is contrary to the basic premise on which the Secretariat is expected to function, but soon destroys whatever influence it might be able to exercise.

The circumstance that such authority must be indirect rather than direct does not in any sense lessen its effectiveness. It must be used with caution, but properly used it can be a valuable aid in serving as a guide and indicating courses of action.

Leadership from the Secretariat presupposes a well organized, well equipped and well directed technical and administrative personnel, possessed of a high sense of responsibility and dedicated to the purposes of the Organization. They must understand that they "have accepted responsibility beyond that of citizens and officials of a single republic." They must have instilled in them the spirit of the international civil servant, able to subordinate national sentiments and prejudices to the international objectives of the Organization.

Leadership cannot be expected from a Secretariat torn by discord and dissension. A poorly organized, badly directed and inefficent Secretariat is a disservice to itself as well as to the Organization. It is a reflection not only on the administration but on the Council as the organ responsible for the proper discharge by the Pan American Union of the duties assigned to it.

The Secretary General of the OAS is a regional counterpart of the Secretary General of the United Nations. It is inconceivable, however, that he would ever be entrusted with the initiative or the authority exercised by the Secretary General of the world organization. Entirely apart from personal qualifications, it is not in keeping with the temperament of the governmental representatives or the conditions under which the inter-American regional system operates, to delegate to any one individual the powers that have been entrusted to the Secretary General of the United Nations.

The Charter of the U. N. and that of the OAS are not too dissimilar in their provisions on the powers and duties of the Secretary General. Both are the principal administrative officers and both are required to submit annual reports on the work of their respective organizations.

The U. N. Charter specifically recognizes the right of the Secretary General to "bring to the attention of the Security Council any matter which in his opinion may threaten the maintenance of international peace and security." Under the Charter of the Organization of American States the Secretary General "shall participate with voice, but without vote, in the deliberations of the Inter-American Conference, the Meeting of Consultation of Ministers of Foreign Affairs, the Specialized Conferences and the Council and its organs." In the exercise of this privilege it must be assumed that the OAS Secretary General has a degree of initiative in determining when he shall speak and what he shall say, and that implicitly at least his authority could be as great and as far-reaching as that of the Secretary General of the U.N. But that is not the way in which the office of Secretary General of the OAS has evolved. His functions have been restricted almost exclusively to the administration of the Pan American Union, and his interventions in Council and conference deliberations have been limited largely to providing secretariat services.

In the U.N. the Secretary General frequently is entrusted with investigations and even with the execution of Security Council and General Assembly decisions of a highly political nature. In contrast, in the OAS fact-finding inquiries to enable the Council of the Organization to function as the provisional organ of consultation invariably have been undertaken by committees made up of members of the Council itself, rather than through the General Secretariat.

The annual report of the Secretary General of the U. N. is not merely a factual presentation of work undertaken during the preceding year; it is also used by the Secretary General as a vehicle for expressing his views on important political issues pending before the organization. In the first few years following the adoption of the Bogotá Charter the Secretary General of the OAS also sought to use his annual report as a medium for commenting on current questions. The reaction of the Council, however, was so unfavorable as almost to constitute a reprimand; so much so that the practice was discontinued and the annual reports have since been limited to a mere factual recital. No Secretary General has since had the temerity to express himself, other than in general and platitudinous terms on any issue of hemispheric importance.

It is a curious anomaly that during the past decade when the Organization of American States was producing the least and while its prestige was in a continuous process of deterioration, the size of its secretariat and its cost of operation were growing to an all-time high. In the bureaucratization of the OAS, Parkinson's Law is substantiated in an outstanding manner.

The Charter of the Organization brought within its framework and created an elaborate structure of organs and sub-organs, of permanent and *ad hoc* agencies, of specialized organizations, of councils, commissions and committees—all with their directing bodies of official governmental representatives and all with their secretariats. So complicated is the mechanism that many of the governments and not a few of those immediately responsibe for its direction are unfamiliar with its ramifications or the interrelationship and interdependence of its various parts.

In the years that have elapsed since the Charter was signed, few of these organs have functioned in the way in which they were expected. As not infrequently happens under such circumstances, new media are set up to investigate the cause of the breakdown and to propose remedial measures that appear to be necessary. The Committee of Presidential Representatives, named in 1956 following a meeting of the Presidents of the American Republics in Panama, and the Committee of Twenty-one appointed in September of 1958 to study "the formulation of additional measures of economic cooperation" are cases in point. There is nothing to indicate that the proposals emanating from these groups have solved any basic issues. What they do reflect is dissatisfaction with the *status quo*. They also afforded justification for adding to the existing superstructure, with the result that there has been a steady, continuous increase in the cost of operations of every one of the agencies of the Organization.

Bureaucracy has an extraordinary capacity to thrive, even under adverse conditions. Every meeting, every committee, every conference, despite the fact that its results are merely a repetition of previous recommendations, invariably serves as a justification for further budgetary increases. To a bureaucrat bureaucracy soon becomes an end in itself. The size of the institution is the sole measure of value, not what it does or how economically it may be accomplished. Like inflation, bureaucracy feeds on itself. It proceeds at a constantly accelerated pace until it can no longer contain itself, or until those who are expected to finance it refuse it further support.

The Organization of America States during the past ten years has experienced an extraordinary growth in size and cost of operations. Inflation has been as rampant here as in the national economies of some of the member states; the inflationary process has been not of the creeping but of the run-away variety.

This growth has occurred principally in the budget of the Pan American Union, reflecting the centripetal forces that have been at work during the past decade, resulting in the centralization in the General Secretariat in Washington of a constantly increasing proportion of the over-all operations of the Organization.

So great has been this process of centralization and bureaucratization that it has created the impression in many minds that the whole Organization has its seat in Washington. Actually, the Organization, as such, has no permanent seat; it is located in every one of the twenty-one member countries, wherever any part of its work is carried on. But when 90% or more of its activities are conducted in or directed from one place, and a corresponding amount of its funds are similarly disposed of, the assumption is understandable, erroneous though it may be, that the permanent seat of the Organization is also located there.

In the last fiscal year before the signing of the Charter, the budget of the Pan American Union was only $850,000, and its personnel numbered 171 employees. Obviously, the pre-Charter budget was too low, and in the first year thereafter the figure was placed at slightly more than $2,000,000. Since then the growth has been not only steady but has proceeded at a constantly accelerated rate. It required five years (1949 to 1954) for the budget of the Pan American Union to grow from $2,000,000 to $3,000,000; three years (1954 to 1957) to jump from $3,000,000 to $4,000,000; only two years (1957 to 1959) to go from $4,000,000 to $5,600,000. In the two years from 1959 to 1961 the budget increased nearly three million dollars more to $8,300,000, and for the fiscal year 1961-62 an additional million and a half dollars have been added bringing the total to just below $10,000,000.

During this twelve year period the staff of the Pan American Union has grown from the 171 that it numbered before Bogotá to 553 at the beginning of 1961, plus an indeterminate number of others engaged on a contract or other temporary basis.

Although the budgets of all the inter-American agencies in the years preceding the Charter were low, it was during that period that the inter-American regional system was making its greatest contribution in consolidating the relations among the American Republics. Never before or since had the unity and solidarity of the American Republics been stronger. Equally interesting is the circumstance that in the area in which the Organization has accomplished the most during recent years — that of peace and security — it has been done with a minimum of cost and of staff. Obviously, progress and achievement cannot be measured in dollars and cents.

Bureaucratic growth and a steadily expanding budget are dangers against which an efficient administration and a responsible Council charged with supervisory control must constantly be on the alert. With that vision and foresight so characteristic of him, the first Secretary General of the Organization, Alberto Lleras Camargo, realized these dangers and warned against them in his first annual report:

"If the Organization of American States does not prove to be effective, economical in operation, and responsible in attitude, but grows in a haphazard fashion, on a basis of good intentions and casual improvisations, as has occurred in the past with similar entities, the day will come when the governments, already under pressure from many agencies of international cooperation, will find themselves unable to meet so easily their financial obligations, and will consider drastic reductions."

Chapter VII

THE UNITED STATES AND THE OAS

In the final analysis, leadership must come from the governments. The Organization of American States is, after all, an inter-governmental institution. To quote again the distinguished first Secretary General, Alberto Lleras Camargo, "the Organization is what the member governments want it to be . . . The governments are the Organization, particularly in the case of ours, where every member has one equal vote in the policy-making bodies."

The Council can, if it will, exercise considerable leadership. It is the medium through which the governments may express their individual views with respect to the Organization, and through which the collective views of the community of American States can best be made known to the governments.

But ultimate authority rests with the governments. This obligation of leadership devolves upon every member, large and small. The history of the inter-American movement is replete with the contributions that individual countries have made. The collective contribution of the Latin American members has been made evident on more than one occasion. The acceptance and incorporation into the international law of the Western Hemisphere of the principle of non-intervention and the inclusion in the Charter of the United Nations of Article 51 recognizing the right of individual and collective self-defense stand as tributes to the interest in and the dedication of the Latin American countries to Western Hemisphere regionalism and solidarity.

But primary responsibility for preserving and building up the inter-American regional organization devolves upon the United States. To say this is not to reflect in any way on the other members. In the same way that in the western world generally the United States is looked to for initiative and guidance, so also in the Western Hemisphere it is expected to set the course and point the direction the regional organization should take. The issue is not the leadership of the United States, but the manner in which that leadership is exercised.

The obligation of leadership devolves upon the United States not merely because we can make the greatest contribution, but also because we have the most at stake. Although the regional system is only one channel through which international relations in the Western Hemisphere are conducted, it has in the past served as a useful medium in giving effect to the foreign policy objectives of all members states, including the United States.

It was we who initiated and sponsored the First International Conference of American States that marked the beginning of the modern Pan American movement in 1890. It is we who have always been its strongest champions. The fortunes of the Pan American movement have always revolved around the United States and its relations with the other American Republics. As these relations prospered so also did Pan Americanism; as they deteriorated so did the inter-American movement.

The interdependence between the inter-American regional system and the relations between the United States and Latin America is strikingly revealed in a comparison of the fortunes of both during the first five decades of the twentieth century.

Between 1900 and 1930, United States relations with Latin America suffered a continuing decline and deterioration. Marked by the Roosevelt corollary to the Monroe Doctrine, under which we assumed the role of guardian with its concomitant practice of unilateral intervention to preserve order and stability; the Wilsonian policy of *de jure* in place of *de facto* recognition of new governments; and the practice of "Dollar Diplomacy" under which we sought to control the fiscal policies of other governments and to use American capital as an instrument of foreign policy, Latin American reaction to these policies and practices tended to become more critical and outspoken. Inevitably this had its effect on the inter-American regional system. First expressed on a limited scale at the Fifth Pan American Conference of Santiago in 1923, criticism reached a climax in 1928 at the Sixth Conference of Havana in a debate on the principle that "no state has the right to intervene in the internal or external affairs of another." The issue was a difference between the United States on the one hand and the Latin American countries on the other, but not a few commentators viewed the Havana conference as marking the end of the Pan American movement itself.

Actually, it marked a new beginning. For it provoked a re-examination by the United States of its Latin American policy and as a result: The Roosevelt Corollary was eliminated from the Monroe Doctrine and that national doctrine returned to its original basic principles; the practice of intervention was abandoned; our recognition policy returned to the traditional criterion of *de facto* control; and finally the Good Neighbor policy was enunciated by Franklin D. Roosevelt. Not only were United States-Latin American relations improved as a result of these changes, but the Pan American movement and the whole system of inter-American relations were transformed and revitalized. Inter-American relations were never more firmly established, and by the time of our entry into the Second World War the unity and solidarity of the American Republics had reached the highest level in history. This sentiment continued to carry over beyond the war years, and culminated in the signing at Rio de Janeiro in 1947 of the Inter-American Treaty of Reciprocal Assistance and of the Charter of the Organization of America States at Bogotá in 1948.

Today, we are at a stage—both with respect to our relations with Latin America and the status of the inter-American regional system —comparable to that of 1928. In the political campaign of 1960 there was considerable debate as to whether the international prestige of the United States was at an all-time high or an all-time low. There can be no doubt in anyone's mind that in so far as our relations with Latin America are concerned, they are not today what they were in 1948, and with that decline there has occurred a corresponding deterioration in the effectiveness of the inter-American regional system. As now organized and functioning, the OAS is not performing the duties entrusted to it or fulfilling the purposes for which it was created. As the author of a recent study prepared for the Senate Committee on Foreign Relations concluded: "The Organization of American States can wither, should it continue to fail in meeting the great expectations of its members."

Whether this situation can be corrected depends upon the kind of leadership the United States is prepared to offer. No nation that pretends to a position of leadership can long neglect its responsibilities without weakening its position and undermining the organization it leads.

Leadership can be expressed in many ways. In no sense does it imply domination. Tactics like the rocket-throwing threats of Nikita Khrushchev have no place among the nations of the Western Hemisphere, where they passed out of style nearly a half century ago with the abandonment of the "Big Stick" policy and the acceptance of the principle of non-intervention. Leadership can be exercised narrowly or broadly, addressing itself only to matters of peculiar interest to us, or encompassing every problem that may be of interest to any member state. It can be expressed most effectively by acting in every respect as a member of the inter-American community, one of twenty-one, prepared to recognize the position and point of view of every other member of the community, and willing to give as much consideration to the problems of the others as we would expect them to give to ours.

Leadership expresses itself in small matters as well as in large. We should not, for example, insist that one American succeed another to an inter-American office when such succession is contrary to the spirit of the Charter and against the express regulations of the Council, as we did in 1958 when the post of Assistant Secretary General of the Organization became vacant. We should not insist that an inter-American agency be established in Washington after a majority of the member states have agreed that it should be located elsewhere, as we did in 1959 when the Inter-American Development Bank was set up in Washington instead of in Caracas. We should not go to extremes in opposing the election of a representative to the chairmanship of an inter-American agency merely because we are not in sympathy with the government of his country, as we did in 1960 to prevent the election of a Cuban as Chairman of the Inter-American Economic and Social Council, a post to which he was entitled by established precedent and which he was eminently qualified to fill. Curiously enough, the representative in question was as much opposed to the policies of Fidel Castro as we were, as evidenced by his subsequent resignation from the Cuban foreign service.

Incidents such as these have no significance in themselves. The issues involved are unimportant, but their cumulative effect is not inconsiderable on the over-all operations of the Organization and in influencing the attitude of the other member states toward us and the Organization.

During the past decade United States interest in the inter-American regional system has been restricted largely to its political features, those relating to peace and security. It is understandable that this should be our primary concern. In fact, the suggestion was once made that the activities of the Organization might be limited to this one aspect, leaving other problems to be dealt with through other media of international negotiation.

But this cannot be. Security is not an absolute condition and its relative position is soon weakened unless it is reinforced by positive accomplishments in other areas. The international community must move forward along all fronts. Only in this way can the security features be consolidated and made even more secure.

It is because of the failure to move forward on other fronts that doubts and misgivings have arisen with respect to the security features of the hemisphere system. It is not enough that the obligation of collective security and reciprocal assistance should be incorporated in a treaty, that this treaty should have been ratified by the 21 member governments of the Organization of American States, or that the principles of the treaty should have met the test of World War II.

What we must now ask ourselves is how secure, how firmly established is this concept of mutual assistance at the present time? Will it meet the test today, as it did in 1942? The experience of 1960, when the Seventh Meeting of Consultation of American Foreign Ministers met in San José, Costa Rica, is not too reassuring on this score. Compared with the position taken by the American Republics in 1954, the decision reached at San José in 1960 represents a weakening of the principle of collective security.

In 1954, at the Tenth Inter-American Conference held in Caracas, the American Republics declared "that the domination or control of the political institutions of any American State by the international communist movement . . . would constitute a threat to the sovereignty and political independence of the American States . . . and would call for a Meeting of Consultation to consider the adoption of appropriate action in accordance with existing treaties." And yet, in 1960, in the face of what we considered to be a direct and positive threat of the international communist movement and its control of the political institutions of an American State, the farthest that the American Foreign Ministers were prepared to go at San José, was the adoption of a resolution condemning such intervention but providing for no "action" to meet the danger.

In his first State of the Union message, President Kennedy set forth as one of the early objectives of his administration: "That our delegates to the OAS working with those of other members, strengthen that body as an instrument to preserve the peace and to prevent foreign domination anywhere in the hemisphere." The political functions of the OAS in preserving peace and security must be strengthened. They are the foundations on which the whole structure rests. If it fails in this area the Organization itself will fail.

The most effective way to strengthen the political features of the regional system is to strengthen its activities in other areas of inter-American endeavor. Whatever may be our primary interest, other member states have theirs, and to the overwhelming majority of them the most urgent problem confronting them since World War II is that of economic development and social reform We must respect that point of view. We must be prepared to collaborate in satisfying the desire and the determination to find solutions to these pressing problems.

In this area, the OAS has done virtually nothing. It is today in the same position in the consideration of the economic and social problems of the Continent as it was twelve years ago. Whether it will do more depends largely upon the United States, the attitude it is prepared to take, the policies it is willing to pursue, and the extent to which it is prepared to utilize the facilities of the multilateral organization in dealing with the economic problems of the other member states. The United States preference for the bilateral treatment of economic problems is understandable. It affords greater flexibility in negotiation and, considering the diversity of the problems that present themselves, many can be dealt with only on a country-by-country basis. But in the interest of strengthening those features of the regional system in which we have a particular interest, we must endeavor to channel through the Organization some of the measures of an economic and social character in which the other members have such great interest and that lend themselves to multilateral treatment.

There is no reason why the nations of Latin America should be grouped together with other countries of the world in matters of economic cooperation, any more than they should be in political matters. In the political area we recognize and share with them regional autonomy to deal with political problems; to determine the measures that should be taken to preserve the peace and assure the security of the Continent. In 1960 we made a special point of emphasizing this concept of regional autonomy both with respect to extra-Continental powers as well as the United Nations. It was likewise reiterated by President Kennedy in his Inaugural address, when he said:

"To our sister republics south of our border, we offer a special pledge—to convert our good words into good deeds—in a new alliance for progress—to assist free men and free governments in casting off the chains of poverty. But this peaceful revolution of hope cannot become the prey of hostile powers. Let all our neighbors know that we shall join with them to oppose aggression or subversion anywhere in the Americas. And let every other power know that this hemisphere intends to remain the master of its own house."

This strongly expressed concept of regional autonomy in the political field should likewise extend to the economic field. Inter-American economic problems, no less than political problems, should be approached within the framework of the inter-American regional system and in the spirit of the inter-American community of states.

"Economic aid" and "economic assistance" are terms that have acquired an unfavorable connotation in the minds of many Americans. They immediately conjure up large outlays by way of gifts, grants and other hand-outs. Whatever form economic relations may take in other sections of the world, that is not the form it should take in Latin America. Economic cooperation extended in this form and with that connotation would be a distinct disservice to the inter-American regional system.

The Latin Americans have repeatedly declared that they are not seeking aid in this sense of the term, and if they were it should not be given them. What they are seeking and what they have a right to expect as members of the inter-American community is adequate consideration of their problems and full participation in solving them in accordance with the principles that have been adopted and the facilities that have been established in the regional organization.

In contradistinction to gifts or grants, the Latin Americans are interested in loans to promote their economic development. The Inter-American Development Bank is a long-delayed but nevertheless welcome manifestation of multilateral economic collaboration. The psychological advantages deriving from its establishment should be as great as the material benefits resulting from its operation.

No less important than loans to the economic security of Latin America is stabilization in the markets and prices of basic commodities. It serves no useful purpose to provide economic aid and financial assistance when the foundations of their existing economies are being undermined by falling prices and declining demand for their staple export products. And here we might well ask ourselves whether we have been as helpful as we might have been in achieving this stability.

Considering the importance of coffee in the economy of so many Latin American countries, is there any reason why we should not have acceded to their pleas several years ago and entered into an inter-American agreement fixing quotas on the importation of coffee into the United States? Our steadfast refusal even to consider such a possibility because it might adversely affect coffee producing areas in other parts of the world, merely had the effect of stimulating the output of an already over-produced commodity, a result that in the long run is not beneficial to the coffee producing countries of Africa and certainly not to those of Latin America. The eventual negotiation of an agreement among the coffee producing countries themselves may have been helpful, but has hardly solved the problem.

Likewise, in adopting national economic policies such as the imposition of quotas on lead and zinc, restrictions on petroleum imports, and tariff increases on wool imports, how and to what extent should we take into consideration the effect that such measures may have on the economies of the other members of the inter-American community? Here again, in dealing with problems of this nature, much more can be done than has been done in utilizing the facilities of the inter-American regional organization.

One of the great achievements of the inter-American system is the development of the procedure of consultation, a practice under which representatives of the several countries meet to consider problems of an urgent nature and of common interest. This procedure has reached its highest expression in the political field, in the realm of peace and security.

The Charter of the OAS contemplates consultation in the solution of economic problems, but no adequate mechanism has yet been devised to give it practical application. It would be a constructive step forward if the representatives of our government in the appropriate agencies of the OAS were to take the initiative in proposing a procedure of economic consultation that would afford an opportunity to consider the effect on other countries of economic measures contemplated by any one of them.

A procedure of economic consultation is almost certain to come in time. Its form and method of operation may differ from that which has evolved in the political field. As in the case of the latter, its inception may be modest. But even a modest beginning, involving only an exchange of views without binding commitments, would be beneficial. It would at least enable the interested parties to set forth their positions, and it would reveal the effects on the economies of all countries of any measure that any one of them may have in contemplation.

What the inter-American regional organization needs above all else is a change in attitude and particularly a change in attitude on the part of the United States. The Inter-American Development Bank and the recently proposed Inter-American Fund for Social Progress are steps in the right direction, but unless we can view our Latin American relations in a proper perspective, it will make little difference in the end result whether we appropriate $500,000,000, five billion dollars or the thirty billions suggested by Fidel Castro.

The weakness of our hemisphere organization in dealing with the problems of the past decade is essentially a psychological one. It is a weakness that expresses itself in an inability to bring to bear upon the economic problems of the present the spirit that was so strongly in evidence during the 1930's and 1940's, when the American Republics were dealing with the essentially political problems of that era; an inability to look at problems beyond the immediate national interests involved and with an adequate appreciation of the over-all interests of the Continent as a whole.

Somewhere, somehow, this all-important quality, that essential ingredient has been lost. Whether it be called the spirit of Pan Americanism or of inter-American unity; whether it be called the policy of the good neighbor, the good partner, or the *alianza para progreso,* is a secondary matter. It is not an element that derives from a name or a slogan; it is a quality that comes from the heart. Secretary of State Dean Rusk, in his testimony before the Senate Foreign Relations Committee following his nomination, spoke of the "intangibles" in our relations with Latin America. President Franklin D. Roosevelt had an extraordinary capacity to appreciate the importance of these "intangibles" and his Good Neighbor Policy was so tremendously successful not merely because of what was done, but the manner and the spirit in which it was done.

The capacity to approach hemispheric problems in the broad perspective of continental needs and aspirations is reflected in the proposal of Operation Pan America by former President Juscelino Kubitschek of Brazil. It is likewise echoed in the suggestion of Governor Nelson Rockefeller for a Pan American Economic Union. Operation Pan America, as President Kubitschek expressed it, is based upon "a comprehensive reappraisal of Pan American ideals in all their aspects and implications." The proposal of Nelson Rockefeller, coming as it does from one who has had vast experience in the field of inter-American relations, is significant for it represents a recognition by a leading political figure of our own country that economic problems, no less than political ones, must be approached from the standpoint of the Continent as a whole—Latin America, the United States and, yes, even of Canada.

No little encouragement with respect to the future of our relations with Latin America and of the inter-American regional system in general, can be derived from the initiatives taken by President Kennedy early in his administration. His pledge to the Republics of Latin America in his first State of the Union message of a "new alliance for progress" and his follow-up request that the Congress appropriate the $500,000,000 for the Fund for Social Progress, offer possibilities of a new era in inter-American relations. No less significant than the proposal itself is the change which it reflects in the attitude of the United States toward the other states of the hemisphere. For the first time in more than a decade and a half we appear prepared to deal with continental problems within the continental framework and in a broad spirit of Pan American cooperation and collaboration.

The task which the Fund seeks to accomplish is a formidable one, and its success depends upon the combined efforts of all countries and all agencies, national and international, public and private. It will not be completed between sunrise and sunset. The ten-year program which the message of the President envisages reveals an appreciation of the magnitude of the job to be done. An effectively conceived and efficiently executed program can accomplish much in a decade, but even then all the objectives will not have been attained.

The $500,000,000 Social Progress Fund is only one part of a larger problem. Land reform and improvements in education, health and housing will not alone suffice. On the contrary, unless accompanied by corrective measures in other areas, such reforms may merely serve to intensify and aggravate the discontent and dissatisfaction that is now so widespread throughout Latin America.

Inter-American activities cannot be grouped into separate watertight compartments. Just as during the decade of the 50's it was a mistake to place too great stress on the political features of the system, so in the 60's it would be a mistake to over-emphasize the social at the expense of the economic. If the Pan American organization is to prosper it must move forward on all levels. Economic development must parallel social reform. There is no little merit in the argument that the former should precede the latter; that social betterment is a consequence of economic progress. Certainly economic development cannot lag behind; the two must at least go forward simultaneously.

Inevitably the question is being asked, what specifically is the United States prepared to do to help solve the economic problems of our Latin American neighbors? To what extent are we prepared to aid them in the stabilization of the markets and prices of their basic commodities? Are we willing to engage in consultations with them whenever national decisions are in contemplation that may have repercussions on their economies, such as tariff changes and the imposition of import quotas? Are we prepared to modify our attitude toward state participation in certain areas of economic development which we have long insisted should be reserved for private enterprise? The answer to these questions will, in the final analysis, be as much a test of the change in attitude as anything that may be undertaken in land use, education, health and housing.

Pan American cooperation cannot be a one-way street. A change in the attitude of the United States toward the basic economic and social problems of the Continent must be reciprocated by the Latin American members of the inter-American community. The responsible leaders of Latin America and those who have traditionally dominated the political, economic and social life of those countries must change their thinking of centuries and their attitude toward the condition of the underprivileged masses. This change of thought and of action will not be brought about easily, it will not occur spontaneously. On the contrary, it will encounter considerable opposition from many who will be asked to give up something to which they consider themselves entitled as a matter of right. Not only must they be made to realize their obligations to the people of their respective countries, but each country must be encouraged to examine the problem of economic and social development not from the narrow standpoint of national self-interest alone but from the broader perspective of the collective welfare of the community of American States.

No program is more effective than the instrumentalities through which it is sought to be implemented. The designation of the Inter-American Development Bank and the OAS as media through which much of the social program is to be carried out has its encouraging features, but it also raises doubts and misgivings. It affords an opportunity to the inter-American regional system to justify its existence and to regain some of the prestige it has lost in recent years. The Inter-American Development Bank, however, has not yet been tested, and its ability to perform is yet to be demonstrated. The record of the OAS in recent years has been a consistent record of failure, and the allocation of $6,000,000 to strengthen the Inter-American Economic and Social Council and its technical secretariat may, on the basis of their past performance, be a further waste of funds. Building layer upon layer on a technical and administrative staff that has shown little capacity in the past to deal with economic and social problems is not the happiest augury for the success of the program in the future. The member states, including the United States, and their representatives charged with responsibility for the effective functioning of the Organization must be prepared to make the institutional and personnel changes that the magnitude of the job requires. It would be a tragedy if, for lack of an efficient secretariat, the new program that appears to be opening should fail of its promising possibilities.

Under the best of circumstances a program of the magnitude and complexity of that envisioned in the *Alianza para Progreso* is difficult to execute. Maximum results can be achieved only with the enthusiastic collaboration of the individual states and the existence of a strong spirit of continental unity and solidarity. In the final months of 1960 and the beginning of 1961 it appeared that these elements were in the process of being recaptured. But by mid-1961, when the first practical step was taken for the implemntation of the program with the appropriation by the Congress of the initial sum of $500,000,000, the outlook had again suddenly changed; the times and circumstances were anything but favorable. Inter-American relations had apparently reached their nadir, politically as well as economically and socially

The United States in particular and the Continent in general were reeling under the impact of the Cuban fiasco of April of that year, an incident that will leave its imprint on the regional organization and affect inter-American relations for years to come. The inter-American regional system appeared to be incapable of functioning in the presence of its gravest crisis. The Eleventh Inter-American Conference, scheduled to meet in Quito, Ecuador, in May, had been indefinitely postponed because the domestic situation in Ecuador itself, plus the boundary controversy with Peru and the generally unfavorable international situation, made the time unpropitious for a meeting of the "supreme organ" of the OAS. Diplomatic relations among many American Governments had been broken, in the case of the Dominican Republic by the collective decision of all and in others by the unilateral action of individual countries. In the light of this combination of ideological conflicts, territorial disputes, and diplomatic breaches, the observation of the Mexican Foreign Minister that the resulting situation "necessarily casts a shadow on continental solidarity" was a masterpiece of understatement.

The Cuban crisis, and the attitude of the United States and of the other American Republics to this problem, emphasizes once again the importance of consistency and continuity, and adherence to basic principles, in the conduct of international relations. Almost from the very outset this country as well as those of Latin America had

been guilty of contradictions and inconsistencies in their approach to
the Cuban problem, of vacillation in the channels of approach,
and above all of a failure to adhere to established principles and to
respect previously accepted commitments. Under such conditions, con⁻
fusion and chaos are almost inevitable.

Inter-American relations, as previously observed, may be dealt
with bilaterally on a country-to-country basis, or multilaterally
through the collective facilities of the inter-American regional system. In a given situation elements may be present that warrant the
use of one method or the other; but the two should not be used in-
discriminately, and to shift from one to the other or to vacillate between the two, is merely to weaken both. It is not possible to ride
two horses at the same time. In the case of Cuba, unfortunately,
that is what was attempted. The Cuban issue has been the object of
collective action through the OAS; it has been the object of unilateral
action by the United States. Thus far neither has succeeded. Perhaps
the failure of each is a consequence of the failure of the other

United States disappointment with the failure of the inter-American
regional organization to deal adequately with the Cuban situation
is understandable Convinced as we were of the growing communist
influence in Cuba, and in the light of the commitment of the
Caracas Declaration of 1954 that the domination of the political institutions of an American State by the international communist movement would call for collective action to consider adoption of appropriate measures, the Meeting of Consultation of American Foreign
Ministers held in San José in August, 1960, was woefully disappointing.
Far from providing action the Declaration of San José merely emphasized the differences among the member states. Inevitably it contributed to the sentiment that found and continues to find increasing
expression in the United States, that a solution must be sought through
direct, unilateral measures.

On the other hand, the unilateral steps taken by the United States
from time to time in its relations with the Castro government gave
support to the Latin American view that the problem was a bilateral
one and not appropriate for continental action. The break in diplomatic relations and the imposition of economic sanctions, fully
warranted though they may have been in the light of the Castro
provocations, merely strengthened this impression. And finally, the
abortive Cuban invasion of April 1961, and the revelations of the
extent of United States involvement, laid us open to the charge of
unilateral intervention. In some Latin American countries this vio-

lation of one of the most cherished institutions of the inter-American regional system posed a more immediate threat than the May Day, 1961 address of Fidel Castro in which he went much farther than ever before in carrying Cuba into the Soviet orbit. The Cuban episode may well become a classic illustration of how international relations should not be conducted.

Consistency is a virtue that must be practiced by Latin Americans no less than by North Americans. On the issue of Cuba the Latin Americans also have been guilty of an unwillingness to conform to established principles or to proceed in accordance with previously accepted commitments: Politics and expediency, rather than conviction and principle, too often have influenced decisions, with the result that not only has the basic problem failed of solution but the very foundation of the hemisphere system has been undermined. The impact of the Cuban social revolution on the minds of the Latin American people engendered a note of caution in the attitude of more than one Latin American government. It encouraged a tendency to play down the danger of communism and to emphasize the principle of nonintervention. Unfortunately, the circumstances surrounding the abortive invasion attempt served to strengthen the noninterventionist sentiment and to lessen the possibility of collective action.

Intervention and nonintervention, collective intervention and unilateral nonintervention must be re-examined. The Latin American emphasis on nonintervention and their determination to preserve this basic principle of the inter-American regional system is understandable. But what the Latin Americans have failed to recognize, or have convenintly ignored, is that the correlative of unilateral nonintervention is collective intervention whenever the peace and security of the Continent are threatened. Both principles originated at approximately the same time and both have followed parallel paths.

The principle of unilateral nonintervention has been reiterated at almost every inter-American conference since it was first accepted in 1933. The principle of collective responsibility for continental peace and security has likewise been reaffirmed at successive conferences since it was first laid down in 1936. The interdependence and interrelationship of the two is recognized in the Charter of the OAS. The oft-quoted Article 15 that "no state has the right to intervene, directly or indirectly, for any reason whatever in the internal or external affairs of another state," has as its counterpart the provision of Article 19 that collective intervention, or "measures adopted for the maintenance of peace and security in accordance with existing treaties, do not constitute a violation of the principle set forth in Article 15."

The dilemma that now presents itself to the American Republics and to the inter-American regional organization is how to reconcile these two principles and make both effective. Does the continued respect for the one depend upon the effectiveness of the other? Does the failure of the principle of collective action warrant a return to unilateral action? In a situation of sufficient gravity the answer to the last question is obvious. No nation would hestitate to act when it is convinced that its national security is at stake. Article 51 of the U. N. Charter, which is the basis of the collective security treaty of Rio de Janeiro, recognizes the right of individual as well as of collective self-defense. The law of self-preservation is stronger than the principle of nonintervention.

In seeking a solution to this dilemma the United States must show an appreciation of the importance that the Latin Americans attach to the principle of nonintervention. For them it is the greatest achievement of the inter-American regional system and they wish nothing to occur that will weaken or undermine it. The Latin Americans, for their part, must assume their share of the collective responsibility for continental security and must show an appreciation of the peculiar nature as well as the gravity of present day international dangers.

Intervention and nonintervention must be re-examined in the light of the changes that have occurred in the three decades since the principle was first accepted. The obligation of collective responsibility must apply to every threat to the security of the Continent. Heretofore it has focussed on direct aggression. It must now be studied to determine how it can be made to deal with the indirect threats and dangers that characterize international relations today. The Caracas declaration of 1954 foresaw the possibility of such dangers, but no effective means of collective action have yet been devised to deal with them.

The issue of unilateral nonintervention versus collective responsibility poses one of the most serious dilemmas ever to confront the American Republics and the hemisphere organization. The failure to solve it may well mean that there will be no principle of nonintervention, no principle of collective intervention. The effect on the inter-American regional system is certain to be far-reaching.

The current state of inter-American relations emphasizes once again the interdependence of politics and economics. The question has been asked previously in this study whether a more enlightened approach to economic and social problems might not have anticipated and avoided many of the political difficulties that today confront the Continent. If the *Alianza para Progreso* had been initiated a decade ago, and if the benefits expected to flow from it had been at work during the past ten years, how much brighter the decade of the 60's would now be. It might have avoided the social upheavals that occurred in Bolivia and Guatemala, and that today are threatening in other countries. Even if it could not have prevented the emergence of a Castro and the convulsions that are taking place in Cuba, the spirit of unity and solidarity among the American Republics generally might well have been sufficiently strong to facilitate collective action to deal with Castro and Castroism.

All this, of course, is hypothetical and speculative. And yet it is unfortunate that two of the significant measures of an economic and social nature taken in recent years were the result of hindsight rather than foresight. The Inter-American Development Bank, so long sought and pleaded for by the Latin American members of the inter-American community, was accepted by the United States only after the unpleasant experiences of Vice President Nixon on his 1958 South American trip. The Act of Bogotá, basis of the *Alianza para Progreso*, was originally conceived and is considered by many Latin Americans as a United States answer to the continental effects of Castroism. How much more advantageous would such measures be, politically as well as economically and socially, if they were to be conceived with foresight rather than hindsight. That is the test of statesmanship!

In mid-1961, as the Continent is about to embark on the massive program of economic development and social reform envisioned in the *Alianza para Progreso*, Pan America is indeed in crisis. It is understandable if the hope that its original announcement aroused should, at the beginning of its practical inception, be tinged with skepticism. And yet, if the OAS has a future it will be found only in the spirit of the *Alianza*, in the pledge contained in President Kennedy's first State of the Union message. Quoted at the beginning of this study, it is repeated again at its close:

"To our sister republics of the south, we have pledged a new alliance for progress—*Alianza para Progreso*. Our goal is a free and prosperous Latin America, realizing for all its states and all its citizens a degree of economic and social progress that matches their historic contributions of culture, intellect and liberty."

On the effective implementation of this pledge may well depend the survival of Pan Americanism and the future of the OAS.

INDEX

Act of Bogotá, 65, 67
Act of Chapultepec, 44
Additional Protocol to the Conciliation Convention of 1933, 46
Advisory Defense Committee, 31
Africa, 21, 22, 88
Agricultural Sciences, Inter-American Institute of, 29
Alliance for progress, 1, 87, 90, 96
American Treaty on Pacific Settlement, 47, 48, 49, 50, 51, 52
Argentina
 Buenos Aires Peace Conference, 46
 Elizalde, Rufino de (Minister of Foreign Affairs), 42
 Inter-American Conference for the Maintenance of Peace, 41
 International Conference of American States, Fourth, 30
 Moreno, Mariano, 42
 Organization of American States, attitude toward, 12-13
 Panama Congress, abstention from, 20
 regional commitments, attitude toward, 42
 Saenz Peña, Roque, 42
Assistant Director (PAU), 35-36
Assistant Secretary General (OAS), 36, 85

Bank, Inter-American Development Bank, 5, 64, 77, 85, 88, 89, 92
"Big Stick" policy, 84
Blaine, James G. (Secretary of State), 27, 40, 45
Bogotá, Act of, 65, 67
Bogotá Pact, see American Treaty on Pacific Settlement
Bolívar, Simón, 8, 17, 19, 20, 40, 75
Bolivia, 60-61, 71
Brazil
 coffee problem, 59
 historical development, 9-10
 Inter-American Conference for the Maintenance of Continental Peace and Security, 38

International Conference of American States, Third, 30, 46
Kubitschek, Juscelino (President), 65-66, 74, 90
Meeting of Consultation of Ministers of Foreign Affairs, Third, 43
Nabuco, Joaquim, 46
Organization of American States, attitude toward, 13
Budget (PAU), 80-81
Bureau of American Republics, Commercial, see Pan American Union.
Bureaucracy, 79-81

Canning, George, 18, 19
Caribbean area, 3, 4, 50, 71
Castro, Fidel, 69, 85, 89
Central America, 8, 20
Chapultepec, Act of, 44
Chapultepec Conference, see Inter-American Conference on Problems of War and Peace.
Charter (OAS).
 consultation, 89
 inter-American regional system, basic instrument of, 52
 mentioned, 44, 47, 48, 68, 72, 74, 75, 76, 84
 Organization of American States, bureaucratization of, 79
 Secretary General, authority of, 78-79
 self-defense, right of, 82
Charter (UN), 11, 78-79
Chile.
 abitration, attitude toward, 45
 Bogotá Conference, Delegate to, 39
 Fifth International Conference of American States, 14, 83
 Panama Congress, abstention from, 20
 Tacna-Arica dispute, 14
 United States, cancellation of President's visit to, 61
Clay, Henry, 19
Coffee, 59, 60, 88-89
Colombia, 7, 9, 12, 20, 32, 59
Commercial Bureau of the American Republics, see Pan American Union.